HUGH OF SAINT-VICTOR

Selected Spiritual Writings

HUGH OF SAINT-VICTOR TEACHING

(*From Oxford MS. Laud Misc.* 409, *folio* 3^v, *a codex formerly at St. Alban's Abbey*). All the figures are correctly depicted in the dress of the canons, an undergarment consisting of a surplice over a tunic of equal length, the whole covered by *cappa* and *caputium* (cloak and hood) of darker material.

HUGH OF SAINT-VICTOR

Selected Spiritual Writings

Translated by

a Religious of C.S.M.V.

With an Introduction by

AELRED SQUIRE, O.P.

WIPF & STOCK · Eugene, Oregon

Wipf and Stock Publishers
199 W 8th Ave, Suite 3
Eugene, OR 97401

Hugh of Saint-Victor
Selected Spiritual Writings
By Hugh of Saint Victor

ISBN 13: 978-1-60608-592-9
Publication date 4/1/2009
Previously published by Harper & Row, 1962

Contents

Abbreviations

A.V. *The Holy Bible* (Authorized Version)

MPG J. P. Migne, *Patrologia Graeca*

MPL J. P. Migne, *Patrologia Latina*

Müller Müller, K. (ed.), *Hugo de Sancto Victore. Soliloquium de Arrha Animae* and *De Vanitate Mundi* (*Kleine Texte für theologische Vorlesungen und Übungen*, no. 123), Bonn, 1913.

Vulg. *Biblia Sacra juxta Vulgatae exemplaria.*

Preface

Hugh of St. Victor wrote three major spiritual works which are devoted to the theme of Noah's Ark. The first, commonly known as the *De Arca Noe Morali*, is translated here in its entirety except for a passage involving an abstruse geometrical argument. The text used here is that of the Rouen edition of 1648 reprinted in Migne's *Patrologia Latina*, clxxvi, cols. 617–80. This has been continuously controlled by the readings of Oxford MS Laud. Misc. 370, a good twelfth-century manuscript from St. Alban's Abbey. The divisions and chapter headings of this manuscript have been used here in preference to those of Migne.

The second treatise on *Noah's Ark*, the *De Arca Noe Mystica*, MPL, cxlvi, cols. 681–704, is variously called *De Pictura Arcae* and *De Reformatione Arcae* in the manuscripts. This is not translated here, though it is discussed in the Introduction. It describes and interprets the Ark in terms of an elaborate three-dimensional, coloured diagram; there is however no need to follow all the details of this in order to grasp the conception that Hugh wishes to convey.

A similar decision has been taken in regard to Books III and IV of the third treatise on *Noah's Ark*. This is the *De Vanitate Mundi*, MPL, clxxvi, cols. 703–40, where Hugh returns to the theme of the two previous works. But the first two books of this treatise did seem to deserve a place in a new selection of Hugh's spiritual writings. Except for a few passages in Book II of the *De Vanitate Mundi* which repeat the thought of the first treatise, this has been translated in full, and the text used is that of Karl Müller.[1]

Two shorter extracts from Hugh's works have been ap-

[1] Hugo de Sancto Victore, *Soliloquium de Arrha Animae* and *De Vanitate Mundi* (*Kleine Texte für theologische Vorlesungen und Übungen*, no. 123), Bonn, 1913.

pended to these longer ones. First, there is a memorable passage on the relation between meditation and contemplation from his unfinished commentary on *Ecclesiastes*, (MPL clxxv, cols. 116–18). And lastly, to illustrate another aspect of his mind, the brief *De Substantia Dilectionis* has been included, its authenticity being guaranteed by the oldest extant list of Hugh of St. Victor's works. For this, the text of MPL cxlvi, cols. 15–18, has been used, where it appears as Chapter IV of the *Institutiones in Decalogum*. But in the manuscripts, for instance Merton College, Oxford, MS A.I.I. fol. 140 R.a., it is however often found in combination with another authentic résumé of the works on the Ark, and it is also thus printed in MPL xl, cols. 843–6.

In quotations from the Bible the Authorized Version has been used wherever Hugh's Latin allows. References have been given to the Vulgate wherever this corresponds closely to Hugh's words and differs from the Authorized Version.

Both the translator and the author of the *Introduction* wish to express their gratitude to Dr. Richard Hunt and Professor J. M. Hussey for the sustained and practical help which they have given with the problems arising out of the production of this volume.

Introduction

by Aelred Squire, O.P.

1. *Hugh of St. Victor's life and influence*

In spite of the immense reputation which Hugh of St. Victor gained during his lifetime and has ever since enjoyed, the only biographical facts about him which it seems possible to place beyond all dispute are the day and year of his death. These are attested by reliable and consistent evidence. A letter of Osbert, a member of the community of St. Victor, written at the request of a certain brother John, gives an eye-witness account of Hugh's last hours, of his gratitude under the trials of sickness and the fervour with which he received the last sacraments in the presence of a gathering of monks, canons, clerks and laymen. It tells of his tears as he kissed his crucifix and how, after calling on Our Lady, St. Peter and St. Victor, he quietly gave up his spirit to God 'on Tuesday, February 11th at the third hour of the day, good and humble, gentle and devout'.[1] Although Osbert does not mention the year in which this occurred, a number of fragments of chronicles and inscriptions on early manuscripts give the year as *anno ab incarnatione Domini MCXLI*,[2] that is to say, in February of the year 1141 calculated, according to prevailing practice, as beginning with the feast of the Annunciation, 25th March. Expressed according to our present system this would make the date of Hugh's death 11th February 1142, which fell, as Osbert says, on a Tuesday.

[1] MPL, clxxv, cols. 162–3.

[2] E.g. *Anno ab incarnatione Domini MCXLI, III idus Februarii obiit magister Hugo S. Victoris canonicus*. *Chronicon Breve* from the abbey of Clairmarais, ed. E. Martène et U. Durand, *Thesaurus novus anecdotorum* (Paris, 1717), III, col. 1385.

Among Hugh's own writings autobiographical references are rare, and the few instances which occur are difficult to evaluate. 'I have been an exile since I was a lad', he says at one point, when he is discussing the qualities of detachment that make a good student.[1] But the whole passage has too bookish a flavour to throw any direct light on the vexed question of his origins save, perhaps, that he was a foreigner in Paris. Wherever he came from, his presence among the Canons of St. Victor is doubtless most correctly seen as part of that general movement towards reformed religious foundations of various types which Robert of Torigni, writing in the fifties of the twelfth century, describes in a short work on the changes in monastic life about the turn of his own century. As one might expect, the account begins in Burgundy with the events which were to have spectacular results in the foundation of the Cistercians, and passes on to the beginnings of the Carthusians and of the monasteries of Fontevrault and Savigny. Robert then continues:

'About the same time, Master William of Champeaux, a very well-lettered and religious man, who had been archdeacon of Paris, taking with some of his disciples the habit of a Canon Regular, began to build a monastery of clerks outside the city of Paris, in a place where there was an oratory of St. Victor the martyr. But being himself raised to the bishopric of Chalons, his disciple, the venerable Gilduin, was made the first abbot there. Under his rule many distinguished clerks, versed in secular and sacred learning, came to live together in that place; among whom, Master Hugh of Lorraine was especially conspicuous both for his knowledge and his humble observance. This man wrote many books, which there is no need to enumerate, since they are available to everyone.'[2]

This short paragraph not only contains almost all we know about the foundation of the Victorines, but also gives us the oldest datable tradition about the region from which Hugh of St. Victor came. Vague though it be, it clearly deserves a rather

[1] *Didascalicon*, ed. C. H. Buttimer (Washington, 1939; always cited from this edition), lib. iii, cap. 19.

[2] *De immutatione ord. monach.*, cap. V (MPL, ccii, col. 1313).

special respect, when considered in relation to other evidence whose true value it is harder to assess. The great Benedictine scholar Jean Mabillon believed that its testimony was not incompatible with an inscription he found at the abbey of Anchin on a twelfth-century manuscript of Hugh's works, which declared that Hugh came from the region round Ypres.[1] As a modern scholar, who has endeavoured to vindicate Mabillon's opinion, has said, the difference between Lorraine and the Low Countries would seem to be no more than the difference between one side of the river Scheldt and the other.[2] It requires however some ingenuity for the many writers who support Hugh's Saxon origin[3] to explain the connexion with Lorraine. Nevertheless, even this has been attempted in the most recent and thorough re-examination of the evidence in favour of this second and perhaps more widely reported view.[4] Whatever may be urged in its defence, it may be doubted how far some of the evidence from German sources can ever be received with complete confidence, but certainly a neglected and most circumstantial entry under 5th May in the fourteenth-century necrology of St. Victor goes far to compensate for the late date at which we first hear of Hugh's having come from Saxony. This entry reads:

'Solemn anniversary of Hugh, priest of happy memory and

[1] *Veterum Analectorum* (Paris, 1675), I, pp. 326–7.

[2] F. E. Croyden, 'Notes on the life of Hugh of St. Victor', *Journal of Theological Studies*, 40 (1939), pp. 232–53. Croyden's views are substantially followed by R. Baron, 'Notes biographiques sur Hugues de St. Victor', *Rev. Hist. Ecclés.* 51 (1956), pp. 920–34. Two manuscripts now at Douai, MS 362 from Marchiennes and MS 363 from Anchin, bear an inscription identical with that printed from a Marchiennes MS by Martène et Durand, *Voyage Littéraire de deux religieux bénédictins* (Paris, 1724), ii, p. 93, and MS 362 is therefore most probably the manuscript which they saw. But there is difficulty in identifying MS 363 with Mabillon's MS, unless he was mistaken not only in giving the date 1142 for 1141, but also in a slight difference of reading. The librarian of Douai has kindly assured me that he believes both inscriptions to be twelfth century.

[3] The entry under *Hugh of St. Victor* in *Oxford Dictionary of the Christian Church*, ed. F. L. Cross (Oxford, 1958) is representative of the biography that goes with this view.

[4] Jerome Taylor, *The origin and early life of Hugh of St. Victor: an evaluation of the tradition* (*Texts and Studies in the History of Medieval Education*, V, University of Notre-Dame, 1957).

archdeacon of the church of Halberstadt, who came to us from Saxony, following in the footsteps of his nephew Master Hugh, canon of our church, and taking the habit in our church, completed a praiseworthy life there. He it was who with notable generosity enriched our house, with gold and silver and precious vestments, carpets and curtains and various other furnishings out of his property. Among his benefactions we wish particularly to record and commemorate the fact that the fabric of this our church was built and completed at his charge and expense.'[1]

Is this tradition—the strongest element in the Saxon case—purely a late invention? It accords with the possibility that the personal tie with several members of the Augustinian community of Hamersleben, near Halberstadt, manifested in the dedication of Hugh's own work *De Arrha Animae*[2] was also a personal tie of some unspecified kind with the house itself. But then it is equally true that, among the twelfth-century documents, the nature of the connexion with Hamersleben has remained an isolated enigma. Until someone is able to produce evidence for the theory of Saxon origin that must undeniably be placed rather earlier than one hundred years after Hugh's death,[3] the possibility that the whole story has gradually been fabricated on the basis of one intriguingly indecisive letter can never be finally excluded. Meanwhile, it would perhaps be wiser to preserve about the whole matter the reticence of Hugh himself, and of his contemporaries.

In any case, Hugh's mature choice of a spiritual home is far more significant for his career. The very physical situation of St. Victor and the antecedents of its founder are suggestive of the special nuance religious life there would develop. We do not know the immediate circumstances which led William of Champeaux to renounce his master's chair at Notre-Dame,

[1] Fourier Bonnard, *Histoire de l'abbaye de S. Victor* (Paris, 1904), I, p. 88, n. 4.

[2] *P.L.*, clxxvi, cols. 951–70. Engl. trans. F. Sherwood Taylor, *The Soul's Betrothal Gift* (London, 1945).

[3] The earliest hint appears to be in the phrase *Dicunt eum natum fuisse de Saxonia* in the chronicle of Alberic of Trois-Fontaines which finishes in 1241 (*Monumenta Germaniae Historica*, Script., 23, 828).

sometime in 1108, and retire across the river to a retreat set against the background of the woods and vines of the Montagne St. Geneviève.[1] But in a letter which he received from Hildebert of Lavardin, it is clear that his ultimate motives are accurately interpreted in the language of the day as being the pursuit of that philosophy of evangelical living which was then inspiring the reformed religious life everywhere.[2] His admiration for St. Bernard of Clairvaux was eventually to lead William's own thoughts further in the direction of a more remote monastic life. But in establishing a house of regular observance at St. Victor, not far from the city gates of Paris, he inevitably created a cloister with a window open on the busy intellectual world which he had intended to leave behind him. It was a place suited to the development of a contemplative life in which real study had a definite part to play.

Bernard, one of the great teachers of the old cathedral school of Chartres, had once said, in words that everyone remembered, 'A humble mind, an enquiring disposition, a quiet life, silent observation, poverty in a foreign land—these are wont to resolve for many the problems of study.' Hugh quotes these lines which seem so aptly to describe the conditions and the ideal a man could hope to realize at St. Victor, and adds that Bernard 'had, I believe, heard the saying that manners enhance learning'. For the canonical life, with its regular hours, controlled by a *matricularius*,[4] its rule of claustral silence, and the urbane simplicity of its common table was calculated to develop virtues that the good religious and the good student might share alike. This life of canons, living in common, had its obscure beginnings in the clerical households of early bishops like St. Augustine at Hippo. His so-called rule, combined with a customary of some kind, was frequently adopted in later centuries by clergy no longer attached to a cathedral, but dedicated, as at St. Victor, to a regular life with a monastic

[1] Fourier Bonnard, op. cit., p. 5.

[2] *Epist.* 1 (MPL, clxxi, col. 141).

[3] *Didascalicon*, iii, 12 (p. 61, lines 11–15).

[4] Cf. *Antiquae consuetudines canonicorum regularium S. Victoris*, ed. E. Martène, *De antiquis ecclesiae ritibus* (Antwerp, 1737) tom. iii, app., col. 739.

end in view.[1] Hugh was at home in a house of monastic observance and its atmosphere pervades his thought. It was natural that a reformer like St. Bernard of Clairvaux should be on friendly terms with such a house. Yet there was an appropriateness of a different kind in the fact that when the theologian Peter Lombard came to Paris for the purposes of study, it was to the hospitality of abbot Gilduin of St. Victor that St. Bernard should think of commending him.[2] After all there had from the beginning been a connexion between St. Victor and Notre-Dame.

If the persuasive letter of Hildebert of Lavardin had the effect of making William of Champeaux resume his teaching during the latter part of his brief stay at St. Victor, it is not quite clear how far from this time onwards there was an open school there. The survival of the report of Laurence, a student, on the lectures of Hugh of St. Victor, corrected each week by the master himself, does however make it certain that enthusiastic pupils from outside did attend his lectures since, as the preface explains, it was partly for their sake that the author had undertaken his task.[3] He sent his completed work to a friend Maurice, a monk at whose insistence he had made a point of seeking out the master whose renown had earned him veneration from afar and the love of one who did not know him. These precious details give us a glimpse of the world of personal relationships responsible for the rapid diffusion of Hugh's teaching. The fact that the oldest extant manuscript of Laurence's report is English[4] has suggested the very plausible identification of its author with abbot Laurence of Westminster, and of his correspondent with Maurice, monk of Durham and afterwards abbot of Rievaulx in Yorkshire.[5] That a more famous

[1] See J. C. Dickinson, *The Origins of the Austin Canons and their introduction into England* (London, 1950).

[2] *Epist.* 410.

[3] Text in B. Bischoff, 'Aus der Schule Hugos von St. Viktor' *Aus der Geisteswelt des Mittelalters*, I (*Beiträge zur Geschichte d. Philos. u. Theol. des Mittelalters*), Supplementband III, 1 (Münster, 1935–), p. 250.

[4] Oxford MS Laud. Misc. 344, fol. 41v–58v.

[5] F. E. Croyden, 'Abbot Laurence of Westminster and Hugh of St. Victor', *Medieval and Renaissance Studies*, 2 (1950), pp. 169–71.

successor of Maurice, abbot Aelred of Rievaulx, had access to a text of Hugh of St. Victor at the time when he put together his first major work, the *Speculum Caritatis*, completed in 1142–3, may now be regarded as certain, since a draft of this work contains at least one substantial verbatim quotation from Hugh.[1] This English interest in the writings of the great master of St. Victor, stretching right back into Hugh's own lifetime, is continuously maintained throughout the twelfth century and on into the thirteenth. Thus we find the great bibliophile, Simon of St. Albans, who is credited by his monastic chronicler with the restoration and reform of the scriptorium there,[2] writing to Prior Richard of St. Victor, probably in the late sixties of the twelfth century:

'By hunting them out wherever we could find them hereabouts, we have gathered together the shorter works of Master Hugh, with the enthusiasm and special care appropriate to writings so highly regarded, and have made several of them up into composite volumes. But since we learn on reliable authority that certain of that memorable man's writings are to be found amongst you which either do not exist beyond the seas or are still rare in this England of ours, we have given the bearer of these present letters brief notes of the works we have here.'[3]

May he, the letter asks, be allowed to arrange for copies to be made of those which he sees they still lack at St. Albans? Simon was elected abbot on 20th May 1167 and died in 1183, so that at least one of the two fine St. Albans volumes of Hugh's works which still exist at Oxford may well be the result of the activities to which this letter refers.[4]

Farther north too, the practical influence of Hugh's ideas can clearly be discerned both in the terms in which the Benedictine

[1] A. Squire, 'Aelred of Rievaulx and Hugh of St. Victor', *Recherches de théologie ancienne et médiévale* (1961), pp. 161–4.

[2] *Gesta abbatum S. Albani*, ed. T. Riley (London, 1867), vol. 1, p. 192.

[3] MPL, cxcvi, col. 1228D.

[4] More probably Oxford MS Laud. Misc. 370, which has been used to control the text of the present translation. Folio 3v of Laud. Misc. 409 is reproduced as the frontispiece to this book.

abbot John of Kelso commissions a treatise on the Tabernacle, and in the manner in which Adam the Premonstratensian canon of Dryburgh executes it.[1] This work, written about 1180, has obvious affinities with Hugh's various treatises on the Ark and in pursuit of essentially the same inspiration, develops in an even more elaborate manner the pictorial possibilities of an allegorical exposition which takes the literal sense of the text as its point of departure. Hugh has thus by now his secure place among the formative scriptural commentators of his century, and a little English thirteenth-century book of notes on the various books of the Bible, in which quotations from him appear together with others from St. Bernard, Aelred of Rievaulx, Baldwin of Ford and Adam of Perseigne, may be cited as typical of the more modest uses of his works in the spiritual and devotional life of English monasteries.[2]

This is only to sketch, in a highly selective manner, the sustained influence in one country alone of an immensely productive teaching career that had gradually assumed European significance.[3]

2. *Hugh's Writings and Teaching on the ascetical life*

The assessment of Hugh's influence in all its ramifications is necessarily a slow and fortuitous business, not only because it is often discreetly hidden, but also for two reasons arising out of the nature of Hugh's work itself. The first is connected with its very form. For it consisted not only of full-length treatises and commentaries, but also of an ever-increasing mass of brief records of the fruits of Hugh's reflections in clearly formulated independent paragraphs or *sententiae*. Even though many of these eventually entered into the making of his larger works, it

[1] MPL, cxcviii, col. 609–796. Hugh is mentioned by name more than once during the work, e.g. col. 697D and col. 726C.

[2] Jesus College, Oxford, MS E.9.

[3] R. Baron gives a survey of manuscripts in continental monasteries in 'Hugues de St. Victor: contribution à un nouvel examen de son oeuvre', *Traditio*, 15 (1959), pp. 223–97, though he unfortunately almost ignores the English manuscripts.

would not be correct to think of them simply as rough notes. They are finished compositions, produced perhaps on occasion to meet the needs of a student, to answer a question, or simply for their own sake. These short pieces are scattered about in innumerable manuscript collections all over Europe. Many of them are, and perhaps for want of adequate criteria to distinguish them, must always remain, on the uncertain fringe of Hugh's authentic writings which, as a recognized body, are at last beginning to take definitive shape out of the confusions of the manuscripts and early printed editions.[1] Fortunately not all, even of the *sententiae*, are subject to these problems, for many are specifically included in a few early lists of Hugh's works which we have every reason to trust. The most important of these is the *Indiculum*, or list of contents, of the four volumes of Hugh's authentic works, which Gilduin, his abbot, compiled soon after the great teacher's death. On the basis of this list, of a twelfth-century list in the Vatican library, and other evidence of subordinate importance, a recent study of the chronology of Hugh's works has taken into consideration 39 treatises, 171 *sententiae*, 23 letters and 10 sermons.[2] This study, whose brevity, lucidity and austerity of judgement seems likely to win for it a large measure of acceptance, has done much to confirm previous datings, to suggest improvements on others, and to draw attention to many neglected relationships between one work and another. In particular this examination makes it seem almost certain that Hugh must have begun to write before 1120,[3] and that throughout his life the steady range of his interests continued unwavering from beginning to end of a career that culminated in the splendid unfinished commentary on Ecclesiastes. It is not really possible to say that Hugh's thought is more markedly mystical either in his youth or in his maturity, since there appear to have been works of this type at all periods. Indeed, one of the factors that makes it possible to

[1] For a view of the situation with regard to the early printed editions see R. Baron, *Science et Sagesse chez Hugues de S. Victor* (Paris, 1957), pp. vii–xlii.

[2] D. van den Eynde, '*Essai sur la succession et la date des écrits de Hugues de S. Victor*', *Spicilegium Pont. Athen. Anton.* (Rome, 1960).

[3] D. van den Eynde, op. cit., p. 207.

attempt to establish a succession in many of his undated writings is the extraordinary continuity of his thought, which makes him return repeatedly to familiar themes and problems, elaborating, clarifying or correcting his treatment of them.

This impressive output, so formidable in the size, range and number of works it involves, has inevitably constituted a second obstacle to a satisfactory appraisal of Hugh's achievement. Easy commonplaces about him abound and are everywhere repeated, but rare are the studies that seem to be genuinely informed with his spirit and, with the possible exception of his biblical exegesis,[1] it may be doubted whether his writings have yet found their true interpreter. Even in this field of scripture, the now widely accepted view of Hugh as a pioneer in the restoration of the study of the literal sense has not remained unchallenged.[2] It may however be questioned how far the ultimate consequences of his forthright assertion of the fundamental importance of the literal sense can well be denied, even if some of its consequences could scarcely have been foreseen by Hugh himself, or consistently exemplified in his own practice.

Hugh's insistence on beginning with the letter is, it may be granted, only one element in his view of the relation of scripture to doctrine. The effect of his views on this subject as a whole on his work as a theologian and a contemplative is still only imperfectly understood. This is probably because the structure of thought which he proposed to erect upon the basis of the historical sense of scripture was in practice of a complexity and subtlety which it is hard for us, at this distance of time, to grasp in synthesis save possibly in one of his moments of intuition which has an archetypal power. We may prepare ourselves to apprehend it by bearing in mind one primary vision of the complete edifice of holy teaching which dominates Hugh's thought. This is expressed in Book VI of his *Didascalicon* which

[1] Undoubtedly the most influential study of recent years is that of B. Smalley, *The Study of the Bible in the Middle Ages* (2nd ed., Oxford, 1952), p. 83ff.

[2] H. de Lubac, *Exégèse Médiévale*, 2ème partie (Paris, 1961), pp. 287–359, would appear to be written largely as a criticism of the position of Miss Smalley.

is absorbed with the notion of that teaching in all its fullness as a spiritual building.

'The foundation and basis of holy teaching is history, from which the truth of allegory is extracted like honey from the comb. If then, you are building, lay the foundation of history first; then by the typical sense put up a mental structure as a citadel of faith and finally, like a coat of the loveliest of colours, paint the building with the elegance of morality. In the history you have the deeds of God to wonder at, in allegory his mysteries to believe, in morality his perfection to imitate.'[1]

Thus are the three senses of scripture to be related to each other. The *Didascalicon* it must be remembered is concerned only with the inception of this work. Its programme is to form the beginner in his habits of reading with a view to the study of scripture on a really sound basis. It is instinct with the conviction that one ought to learn everything, that nothing is superfluous and nothing in the world sterile, a conviction that remains with Hugh to the end of his days, though it would be possible both from the *Didascalicon* and from other works of his to quote passages that seem to belie this generous and open-minded spirit. It is true that for Hugh everything is ultimately to be subordinated to the contemplative life, and that consequently he takes for granted, even about learning, a traditional western and monastic asceticism. But his acute awareness of the impermanence and defectability of created things, and of the limitations of human knowledge about them, does not lead him to the rejection of the proper uses of the mind. This is as clear from his own practice in the commentary on *Ecclesiastes* as it is in earlier expressions of his thought. If the conviction is particularly prominent in the *Didascalicon* that it is worth taking trouble even about things which may not seem in themselves worth while for the immediate purposes of the exegete, this is largely because the atmosphere of this work is dictated by a concern for *lectio divina*, or holy reading, as pertaining to knowledge, and deliberately leaves aside *meditatio*, with its strongly moral connotation, for another occasion. Meditation, Hugh

[1] *Didascalicon*, vi, 3 (p. 116, line 20).

says, is a very subtle matter,[1] and subtlety, in the most favourable sense of the word, is certainly the mark of the admirable and attractive little work *De meditando* which was possibly intended to fill this gap.[2]

But the student also experiences the need for an introduction to the body of doctrine which is an essential preliminary to the *secunda eruditio*, or higher learning, of allegory. For as Hugh has said in the *Didascalicon*, the two disciplines are very different. 'History follows the order of time, while for allegory the order of knowledge is more to the point, for teaching ought always to start, not from the obscure, but from the evident and better known.'[3] The *De Sacramentis* is Hugh's response to this pedagogical need, a systematic theology whose importance in the evolution of the teaching of that science is as widely acknowledged as that of his earlier work for the study of the Bible. But in Hugh's mind both the *Didascalicon* and the *De Sacramentis* are only instruments. The first helps to lay the foundations of the structure of holy teaching, the second to begin to erect the fabric. The finished work must be sought elsewhere.

It is naturally to be found, not in a book, but in a living experience. Hugh himself strives to realize this experience through those meditations whose concern is 'to detect all the movements that arise in the heart, and see whence they come and whither they are going', whose function is 'judge between day and night, and day and day'.[4] But this is not to say that the experience is so personal that it cannot be spoken of objectively. And when on one occasion, in a discussion with his fellow religious, he is drawn into doing so, it is natural that his mind should return to the notion of a structure as most aptly expressing what he has to teach. This time he finds the perfect structure in a text of scripture itself.

Hugh was to devote three major works and one brief *sententia*[5] to the typology of Noah's Ark, and the fact that each of

[1] *Didascalicon*, vi, 13 (p. 130, lines 9–10).
[2] *De meditando* (MPL, clxxvi, cols. 993 ff.).
[3] *Didascalicon*, vi, 6 (p. 123, lines 10–13).
[4] MPL, clxxvi, col. 995C and 996B.
[5] *Quod amor sit vita cordis* (MPL, clxxvii, cols. 563D–565A).

the major works refers specifically to the other makes it possible for us to place them in the order—*De Arca Noe Morali, De Arca Noe Mystica, De Vanitate Mundi.* The second of these works includes a list of the popes which ends with Honorius II, a contemporary of Hugh, who was pontiff from 1124–30. It would therefore seem that the work may have been written somewhere between these years, perhaps towards the end rather than the beginning of the pontificate.[1] It would probably be reasonable to suggest the period 1125–31 for the composition of all these works. The *sententia* is harder to place. It seems however to presuppose the larger works for its full intelligibility, and also to be linked by its opening phrases with various pieces devoted to the subject of charity which appear to come towards the end of Hugh's life. It may therefore be fairly late.

The reason why Hugh is so haunted by this recurrent theme seems to emerge most clearly in the first of the great trilogy, the *De Arca Noe Morali.*[2] God dwells, he says, in the human heart in two ways, namely by knowledge and by love. Knowledge erects the structure of faith, love embellishes the building with virtue as with an adorning colour. 'Now therefore enter your own inmost heart, and make a dwelling-place for God. Make Him a temple, make Him a house, make Him a pavilion. Make Him an ark of the covenant, make Him an ark of the flood; no matter what you call it, it is all one house of God.' Having said so much, he suddenly sees all the types of spiritual perfection converging upon the engraced and enlightened soul, in whom and for whom all the figures of scripture are designed to be fulfilled, and he bursts into a passage of rare inspiration in which all these signs and symbols of divine fostering and protection, drawn indifferently from the Old and New Testaments crowd into his mind. 'God is become everything to you, and God has made everything for you. He has made the dwelling, and is become your refuge. This one is all, and this all is one. It is the house of God, it is the city of the king, it is the body of Christ, it is the bride of the Lamb. It is the heaven, it is the

[1] 1128–9 (D. van den Eynde, op. cit., p. 80).

[2] For convenience the treatises are referred to by their conventional names.

sun, it is the moon, it is the morning star, the daybreak and the evening. It is the trumpet, it is the mountain, and the desert, and the promised land. It is the ship, it is the way across the sea, it is the net, the vine, the field. It is the ark, the barn, the stable and the manger . . . the flock and the shepherd, the sheep and the pastures. It is paradise, it is the garden, it is the palm, the rose, the lily'—fountain, river, door, dove, pearl, crown, sceptre and throne—'It is the table and the bread . . . And, to sum it all up, it was for this, with a view to this, on account of this, that the whole of scripture was made. For this the world was created. For this the Word was made flesh, God was made humble, man was made sublime.'[1]

This would seem to be for Hugh a fundamental intuition, the finest concise expression of his conception of Christian wisdom, once its real meaning can be elucidated and grasped in more prosaic and tangible terms. The ark is only one, and that the most apt for his purposes, of all the types of the finished work of theology. For this reason he returns to it on three distinct occasions in works spread over the middle period of his creative activity which are, it seems clear, taken for granted in the brief *sententia* which may well be his last adumbration of this theme.

It is in these three works, considered as a group, that we may, in many ways, most conveniently study how Hugh himself handles the three senses of scripture, historical, allegorical and moral, which are like the six-winged seraphim covering the head and the feet of the One who surpasses all understanding.[2]

Their ultimately moral and spiritual purpose enables us to appreciate the tension between his conception of history in scripture and his experience of it in life, to see with what pains he lays his historical foundations, the real theological effort that goes into his allegorical development, the insight he brings to bear upon the realization, as an interior reality, of the deliverances of faith. Nothing could be more erroneous than to dismiss these as works which juggle with images more or less

[1] See below, *Noah's Ark*, Bk. I, ch. 6.
[2] See below, *Noah's Ark*, Bk. I, ch. 10.

as they please. Hugh's strength and importance as a writer lies in his integral view of Christian life and thought. However remote some of its detail may seem to us now, his, like the finest Cistercian spirituality of this immensely creative twelfth century, is a mysticism which is essentially biblical and theological. In Hugh's case this result is arrived at not merely by instinct but also by design. His theory not only permits but even encourages him to experience a rebirth of images. 'But look what has happened. We set out to talk about one ark and one thing has so led to another that it seems now we have to speak not of one only, but of four . . . The first is that which Noah made, with hatchets and axes, using wood and pitch as his materials. The second is that which Christ made through His preachers by gathering the nations into a single confession of faith. The third is that which wisdom builds daily in our hearts through continual meditation on the law of God. The fourth is that which mother grace effects in us by joining together many virtues in a single charity.'[1] And the propriety of all this, in which the scriptural figure is seen as the type first of the visible Church, and then of the reintegrating character of virtuous endeavour, which culminates in the gratuitous completion of charity, is stated thus: 'There is in some sense only one ark everywhere, for there is only one common ground of likeness everywhere, and that which is not different in nature ought not to be denoted by a different name. The form is one, though the matter be different, for that which is actualized in the wood is actualized also in the people, and that which is found in the heart is the same as that which is found in charity.'[2] This is not just a piece of Platonist philosophy, using Christian imagery, though it is true that Platonism has coloured the manner of thinking from which this kind of exegesis ultimately derives. It is the language which is proper to a world of living symbolism.

What, in fact, is Hugh's picture of the world? Plainly enough it is a world in which the realities expressed in the history and imagery of scripture are operative forces, and the context in

[1] See below, *Noah's Ark*, Bk. I, ch. 11. [2] Ibid.

which they work themselves out is determined by the doctrine of original sin, in terms of which the Christian interprets his own inner experience. The starting-point of the first of the treatises on the ark is one of those monastic discussions which in other twelfth-century works are often developed within the convention of the Ciceronian dialogue. But where he departs from continuous exposition, as he does with the opening of the *De Vanitate Mundi*, Hugh has a preference for the Augustinian soliloquy.[1] At the opening of the *De Arca Noe Morali*, however, the topic of discussion which has occasioned the work is quite simply stated as having been the problem of the instability and restlessness of the human heart. The cause of this instability is traced to the divided desire that results from original sin. Man is seen, as it were, with his inner life turned outwards. In losing his original integrity, banished from the face of the Lord and smitten with the blindness of ignorance, man comes forth from the inner light of contemplation to roam the earth as a vagabond seeking to satisfy his disordered desires. The basic problem of the human situation is thus seen as the problem of right and wrong loves. But although the problem is formulated in this way from the very beginning, it cannot really be said that its solution in terms of the gradual invasion of the soul by charity —which is, indeed, present in these treatises—ever achieves quite the prominence that it does in the works specifically devoted to that subject written during Hugh's latest period. Their doctrine is consequently a necessary complement to the earlier works in any complete view of Hugh's spiritual teaching.

In the Ark treatises it is rather the problem and its more negative implications that are stated with telling force, and this statement takes the form, perhaps most vividly in Book II of the *De Vanitate Mundi*, of what can only be described as a positive terror of time and the time-bound. It is true that the immediate personal impact of this experience is somewhat mitigated by the atmosphere of literary artifice which characterizes the five cautionary tales with which the *De Vanitate Mundi* opens. While not lacking in a certain narrative charm, these

[1] The *De Arrha Animae* is another example.

stories in which apparently happy people come to inescapable disaster are, it may be thought, too remote from reality to achieve an altogether serious philosophical purpose. Indeed, the one on married life is so uncompromisingly pessimistic that the reader who is not scandalized by it, is likely to find it even humorous. The ruthlessness of time is, nevertheless, a thought that returns too often in Hugh to be a mere convention. It recurs like an obsession and, even when he explicitly rejects the old pagan myth of the eternal return in his late commentary on *Ecclesiastes*,[1] it may be doubted if he effectively refutes it. It is perhaps too close to an account of time as he himself experiences it. For it is difficult to take in a wholly impersonal sense the rhapsodic language about time with which Book II of the *De Vanitate Mundi* begins:

'O stream that fails not, O watercourse never still, O whirlpool never sated! Whatever is subject to birth, whatever involves the debt of mortality, that does insatiable death gulp down. It never ceases to consume the one and ensnare the other, or to engulf them both. The present is always passing on, the future always following . . . The mind is never surfeited with desire, but follows the path of the days that are gone, and sees within itself the way by which it too must pass, the end towards which it is moving.'

This is a mood which perhaps came naturally to a man who reveals himself primarily as an intellectual and whose crowded and busy life, never far from strains and controversies can seldom have been free of temptations to yield to those evils of *afflictio* and *occupatio*[2] of which he speaks so discerningly when he is writing about meditation.

It would however be misleading to isolate this existential element in his thought. It is for him only one aspect of the revolution of the ages, for, as he was to say later in his commentary on *Ecclesiastes*, the wisdom of God rules the confusion

[1] MPL, clxxv, cols. 144 ff.

[2] Hugh defines *afflictio* as the state when one becomes impatient with useless interruptions, and *occupatio* as the agitation produced by the immoderate pursuit of valuable purposes. (MPL, clxxvi, col. 116D.)

of experience, 'and what is confused to us is not so to him'.[1] It is in those intuitive opening pages of his first treatise on the Ark that Hugh was to perceive that, 'as the ages in their course return upon themselves, they seem by their cycles to mark out as it were the enclosure of a temple', in which God is sitting, as Isaiah saw him in his vision, as though on a throne. When the prophet says of this seated figure that 'the things that were beneath it filled the temple', the phrase is to be taken 'as denoting that all the periods of time are full of the works of God, and that every generation tells of his wonderful acts'.[2]

But this is to anticipate, and before he proceeds Hugh was first to establish his vision on the basis of a literal exegesis of the biblical account of the construction of the Ark. Its high seriousness is emphasized by the fact that, in addition to making his own contribution, by observation and conjecture, to the views of Origen and Augustine, he permits himself a geometrical diversion to illustrate the beauty of the Ark's proportions. It is, however, fortunately not necessary to grasp this complication in order to follow the argument of the treatise. He regards this section as an optional enrichment of our appreciation of the symmetry of this divinely designed construction. The presence of such a passage in a work of this kind is characteristic of Hugh, and shows how little his esteem for the spiritual interpretation of the text inhibits his intellectual curiosity.

His highest endeavours are, however, reserved for the allegorical exposition of the Ark as a figure of the Church. It is here that he reduces the flux of history to an intelligible pattern by showing the relationship of the redemptive work of Christ to each period of time. His notion that the three phases of natural law, written law and grace are divided into six periods, of which the sixth, the age of senility, is now upon a course of unknown duration, derives from Augustine. But the notion that the Church was founded when the world was founded, and that the men of all periods can have a relationship to the period

[1] MPL, clxxv, col. 145D.

[2] See below, *Noah's Ark*, Bk. I, ch. 8.

of grace which makes them members of the Church, is an independent return to an older patristic tradition such as we find in Origen, whose influence is clearly discernible in Hugh's way of expounding these matters. Perhaps the firmest and clearest statement comes in the second of the treatises on the Ark, the *De Arca Noe Mystica*.

'If the Ark signifies the Church, it follows that the length of the Ark is a figure of the length of the Church. But the Church's length is to be seen in the duration of the successive periods of her history, just as her breadth is in the multitude of the peoples she includes. For the Church is said to widen when the number of her believers is increased, and many are gathered to the faith; while her length consists in that prolongation in time whereby she reaches out of the past, through the present into the future. This length of hers in time is from the beginning of the world to its end. For Holy Church started in her faithful ones from the beginning, and will last until the end of time. We believe, indeed, that there is no period from the beginning of the world until the end of time in which believers in Christ will not be found.'[1]

In his first treatise on the Ark, Hugh has promised to give a pictorial illustration to support and, in a certain sense, to embody his argument, and during the course of the work he does indeed describe two of its elements, an enthroned majesty and an Ark into which he works representations of the Tree and the Book of Life, and the entire contents of the Bible. But his conception is not worked out in its full and bewildering complexity until the second treatise, which in many of the manuscripts is simply called 'the picture of the Ark', and is linked with a paragraph omitted from the printed editions, which Hugh himself may well have written upon completing this second and complementary treatise.[2] It is a treatise which does not make easy reading, for it is an elaborate description of the Ark as a three-dimensional figure which somehow contains the whole of biblical and ecclesiastical history, including portraits

[1] MPL, clxxvi, col. 685B.

[2] This passage has been included in the present translation.

of all the popes from St. Peter to Honorius II, and innumerable divisions and inscriptions, together with ladders representing the ascents from vice to virtue. But the whole culminates, for those who have the will to get there, in a splendid coloured vision rather like the great tympanum of a cathedral, in which a Majesty surrounded by angels sits enthroned, his arms expanded so that they seem to contain everything. In his hand he holds a sphere, within whose first concentric circle the heavens with the signs of the zodiac are depicted. Within that, another circle, representing the air, contains the personifications of the four seasons and the twelve winds. And finally within that, an innermost sphere encircles a map of the world whose extremities coincide with the dimensions of an Ark so orientated as to illustrate Hugh's theory that the sequence of historic periods from Adam corresponds to a geographic movement of the centre of historic interest from East to West.

The whole thing is, one may say, in modern psychological language, a kind of mandala. It both expresses and objectifies an inner experience of the world of scripture and theology and suggests how one may begin to make such an experience an interior reality. The principles upon which this final stage of Hugh's spiritual endeavour work out are probably most clearly explained at the beginning of Book II of the first treatise on the Ark.

'We must distinguish what we are now about to say of the Ark of wisdom from those things which, according to the allegorical sense, we have already applied to the Church. What we showed there in the sphere of existence is here being investigated in the sphere of thought. For things have their own kind of being in the mind of man, where even those which in themselves are either past or still to come can coexist. And in this respect the rational soul bears a certain likeness to its maker. For as in the mind of God the causes of all things exist eternally without change or temporal differentiation, so also in our minds things past, present and future exist together by means of thought. If then by the regular practice of meditation, we have begun to live in our own hearts, we have already after a certain manner ceased to belong to time, and, like men dead to the world, begun to live an inner life with God. We shall then easily make light of any external trials of fate, if our desires are fixed where we cannot be subject to change, where we do not sigh for the past, anticipate the future or fear any difficulty. Let us, therefore, have upright, profitable and pure thoughts, for these are the material from which we shall build our ark. These are the timbers that float on water and burn when put in the fire.'

The three treatises on the theme of the Ark are concerned with both these aspects of the properties of wood, but primarily with the first, that it will float upon the moving flux of time. In the latest of the three, the *De Vanitate Mundi*, which also gives us the most elaborate conspectus of saving history,[1] it is especially evident that Hugh is concerned to establish a point of view from which the passage of time, and the storms and toils of events, can be regarded with tranquillity. Thus, at the end of Book II of this treatise he describes how, if we start out at Adam's end of the Ark and begin to walk, 'we shall find a path that takes us through the midst of the years so that, as we pass along, everything to left and right can be seen on either hand, as if it were done outside in the flood', that flood in which all those who love the world go down with the things to which they cling.

It is in terms of this image of the Ark floating upon the waters that Hugh works out a fresh and original treatment of the ascetic problem of the relation between action and contemplation in Book II of the *De Arca Noe Morali*. He has a simple point to make which is of primary importance for the contemplative life, and it is symbolized by the difference between the position and the function of the door and the window in Noah's Ark.[2] The heart, which cannot in this life be wholly contemplative has, as it were, two kinds of exit: action, to which it goes out by the door in the side of the Ark; and

[1] Books III and IV not only give a summary of the entire Old Testament, but go on to the times of the early martyrs and Fathers.

[2] See below, *Noah's Ark*, Bk. II, ch. 3.

contemplation, to which it rises like a bird through the window in the roof. Now the difference between these two exits, once the Ark is afloat, is that while the window can be opened from the inside with impunity, this is not true of the door. For, just as it was not Noah who shut and opened the door of the Ark, but God who did it from the outside, so involvement in external activity leaves the heart's integrity unimpaired only when the constraint of some genuine necessity opens the door to it. Hugh's *necessitas*, like Augustine's in similar contexts, explicitly includes that pressure of natural need to eat and take air and exercise which is common to all bodily existence, but he has principally in mind the vocation to succour the spiritual necessities of one's neighbour which providential circumstances may require. Like the contemplatives of every generation, Hugh believes that the response to this vocation ought always to mean making a real sacrifice of a life for which a strong spiritual preference is felt, and that only thus can the purity of its motivation be preserved from disordered inner compulsions of pride and ambition.[1] Not that he has overlooked the possibility of the pride of the contemplative life itself which makes it good for a man sometimes to have to learn by the experience of having some external charge thrust upon him, how difficult it is to be bound by one's duty to look after such matters, without giving up the desire for the inner life.[2]

In the process of man's reintegration, which it is the purpose of the contemplative life to achieve and defend, the figure of Christ is central from the very moment of conversion. For the contemplative life is the search in faith for the lost vision of God which was mirrored at man's creation in the human heart. Since then, by being made in his maker's image, Christ, God's eternal life and wisdom, was hidden in man's depths like the treasure in the field of the parable.[3] However, just as man's turning from God was a free act, so too must his conversion be, a conversion whose remotest beginnings are at the same

[1] See below, *Noah's Ark*, Bk. II, ch. 4.
[2] Ibid., Bk. III, ch. 10.
[3] Ibid., Bk. IV, ch. 7 and cf. Bk. III, ch. 6.

time a gift of grace, enabling the desire for its healing to be awakened in the soul as a result of its experience of itself. This is a long and complex process, in which the soul is both active in its efforts to acquire the virtues, and passive to its formation under trials of various kinds, a process in the course of which it needs, as it were, to read the explanation of what is happening to it in the books which God has provided. This is the function of its reflections upon God's double work of creation and re-creation, to use Hugh's habitual manner of distinguishing the two phases of the work of divine providence. The soul's exits through the window of its thoughts upon the work of creation are profitable to it to the extent that they generate in it a salutary fear of its situation in separation from God. They will be profitable too if they produce a distaste for everything transitory by comparison with the One for whom it thus begins to feel the first stirrings of love. Turning to the scriptures and the examples of the saints likewise does it good if admiration leads to imitation, and imitation to the acquisition of the virtues, which are more and more dominated by charity, the crowning virtue that makes us desire and seek Christ, and so unites us to God. For the Incarnate Saviour is both our model in his human nature and the medicine of our souls in his divinity, the Tree and the Book of Life. He is the Book of Life since 'the whole divine scripture is one book, and that one book is Christ, for the whole divine scripture speaks of Christ and is fulfilled in Christ'.[1] He is also the tree of life planted in the midst of the Church by his Incarnation, the source of sacramental grace which, in its turn, is the means whereby that Tree may spring up in the hearts of the saints, as in an invisible paradise.[2] This tree is thus seen as reaching up to heaven through every stage of progress and degree of perfection, as it might be a column in the centre of the Ark, intersecting the floors at each level and carrying the roof beams as, like the unifying virtue of charity, they incline inwards towards their central support.

'The Ark leans on the column, and his Church leans upon

[1] See below, *Noah's Ark*, Bk. II, ch. 11.

[2] See below, *Noah's Ark*, Bk. II, ch. 15.

Christ, for undoubtedly she could not stand at all if he did not hold her up, according to that word in the Canticle: Who is she that comes up radiant from the desert, leaning upon her beloved? Again, just as the column is the measure of the height of each floor, so Christ gives to each one his measure of virtue and progress. And as it divides the different compartments, so Christ at his good pleasure divides the gifts of his graces in Holy Church, making some prophets, others apostles, yet others evangelists, and all the other different functions that have a share in spiritual gifts. So too, as the column is always in the central position, our Lord Jesus Christ has said: Wherever two or three are gathered together in my name, there am I in the midst of them. If, then, we are so weak as to be unable to go up to the third or second floor, let us not lose heart, but let us be gathered together by faith in his name that we may at least be on the ground floor, in the unity of the Church. There let us hold true and unshakeable faith and he will come to us, that he may stand in our midst to praise our good beginning, while being ready at the same time to help us to rise to higher things, that he may be one in all, one among all, one above all, even Jesus Christ our Lord.'[1]

There is a special value in thus laying bare the structure of these treatises in separation from a wealth of subordinate detail. It becomes easier to appreciate how they develop with the logic of images and symbols derived from and rooted in a genuine apprehension of the scriptures, and to understand why Hugh of St. Victor's writing, whatever its occasional lapses and conventionalities, is never far from the living waters. His is also a mysticism fundamentally Christian and sacramental for, as he was to say in a comment on the meaning of the name of Christ which occurs in a later work: 'He called you by his own name, that the memory of him should ever be with you. He wished you to share in his name, and share in its reality, since he anointed you with that same oil of gladness wherewith he was

[1] *De Arca Noe Mystica* (MPL, clxxvi, col. 684CD). MS Laud. Misc. 370, fol. 47v shows that Hugh was using the Septuagint version of the text quoted from the Canticle, which is accordingly translated here.

himself anointed, that the one who is called Christian after Christ, should also be anointed by the anointed one.'[1] In some ways the first two treatises on the Ark are too rich in insufficiently explored lines of thought, and at one point in the second of them Hugh specifically refers his reader to another earlier work for a fuller development.[2] Yet, considered in conjunction with the *De Vanitate Mundi*, no group of Hugh's treatises enables us to see so well how the elements of his teaching on the spiritual life fit together. Nor is even the first of this group lacking in those marks of spiritual maturity which we find again in the latest period of Hugh's writings. Thus, for instance, the long chapter ten of Book Three, which deals with the role, under divine providence, of temptation and trial as a factor in spiritual growth, is not afraid of the notion of the *felix culpa*, the fortunate fault,[3] whereby God permits a serious fall to reawaken the soul to the realities of its situation and return to the love of God, though the idea may be 'difficult to understand and harder to explain'.

It is chiefly in the systematic treatment of the virtues and vices that the most notable developments and refinements are still to come. Thus, although the radical opposition pride-humility is implicit in all three treatises, and in the second, three of the four cardinal virtues, temperance, prudence, and fortitude, are mentioned in connexion with the ladders of ascending virtue, there is as yet no hint of the scheme of the seven deadly sins, or principal vices, which we shall find later in the *De Sacramentis*.[4] A short work *On five groups of seven*, which must belong to this later period, relates this scheme to the remedial effects of the seven petitions of the Lord's Prayer, the seven gifts of the Holy Ghost, seven virtues and seven beatitudes.[5] There is however a more modest allusion to the same scheme in a brief *sententia*, *On the desert of the heart*, which

[1] *De Arrha Animae* (MPL, clxxvi, col. 963D).

[2] The *De Tribus Diebus* is referred to in the *De Arca Mystica* (MPL, clxxvi, col. 693D).

[3] Cf. *De Arrha Animae* (MPL, clxxvi, col. 962D).

[4] *Lib.* ii, pars xiii.

[5] *De quinque septenis* (MPL, clxxv, col. 405 ff.).

particularly deserves notice as incorporating it with an image of the soul's desire of God, which Hugh also uses in his first Ark treatise and finally with greatest effect in the last of all his works. It admirably illustrates how charming these short pieces can be. It is presented as a commentary on the text from the Canticle: *Who is she that comes up from the desert like a column of smoke, aromatic with myrrh and incense and every spice of the perfumer?* 'The good heart is a desert in that it is far from uproar and disturbance, untrodden by the commerce of earthly thoughts. But it is ever green and blossoming, bearing shoots of the virtues. The Holy Spirit, the Dove, sings there, and the voice of man is not heard or anything of his deeds. The column is straight and slender, long drawn-out. It must be straight, for it is so strongly inclined to rise up: and slender, for narrow is the way, drawn-out, for the way is long. Again it is not a column of wood, dead and hard, but of smoke, which has form without substance. For it seems to be something at first sight; but touch it, and there is nothing there. So too every good man seems to be in this world after the appearances of the flesh; but he is not here in affection. Again, smoke goes up from fire, for desire comes from love. And what kind of smoke is it? *Aromatic with myrrh and incense and every spice of the perfumer.* The perfumer is Christ, the aromatic spice the virtues, myrrh mortification of the flesh, incense the heart's devotion. Every spice of the perfumer is the host of all the virtues. It says in the book of Job: *He smells the battle from afar, the urgings of the captains and the clamour of the army.* For the host of the vices has its king or its queen, has its captains, its people, its army. The queen is pride, the captains the deadly sins, the army all their evil consequences. First, then, the captains of the vices make as it were an exhortation to battle, for they deceive a man about what has to be done, and then the army rushes in as with a shout. For once the first suggestion has been accepted, the crowd of vices following makes a charge against the deluded mind with violence and din. So too, of the virtues the queen is humility, the captains the chief virtues, the army every good thing. And when the chief virtues are welcomed by a man with a certain understanding, every good thing soon follows as a matter of course. Here, therefore, he puts first the captains, myrrh and incense, and afterwards the army, every spice of the perfumer.'[1]

The section about the vices in this passage is of course only an adaptation of part of a long commentary of Gregory the Great,[2] of whom Hugh speaks so warmly at the end of the *De Vanitate Mundi* as being full of the spirit of Another, 'with many lovely things to offer, and the delights of truth'.[3] But Hugh is, generally speaking, conspicuously free and bold in his use of his patristic sources, and when he comes to explore the various aspects of the crowning virtue of charity towards the end of his career, we shall find him using the Augustinian conception of the tension between cupidity and charity in an entirely personal way in a short work, the *De substantia dilectionis*, which is included in the following selection. Its opening words seem to suggest that it forms only one of a series of works on the same theme, stimulated, perhaps, in part by the widespread interest in the whole topic of love, human and divine, in both monastic and secular circles in Hugh's own day. For according to the beginning of the short *sententia* in which the image of the Ark recurs: 'The life of the heart is love, and therefore it is quite impossible that there should be a heart that desires to live without love.'[4] The conflation of this *sententia* with the *De substantia dilectionis*, which sometimes occurs in late manuscripts is not altogether inappropriate, but it seems possible with greater confidence to associate the latter treatise with the group of works on charity which may be regarded as culminating in the justly renowned work the *De Arrha Animae*.[5]

This group of works is rich in new ideas and fresh presentations of old ones. They bring down to the level of personal experience the notion (also occurring in the first treatise on the

[1] MPL, clxxvii, col. 539C–540A.

[2] *Moralia in Iob, lib.* xxxi, cap. 44–5 (MPL, lxxvi, col. 619–21).

[3] MPL, clxxvi, col. 739A.

[4] MPL, clxxvii, col. 563D.

[5] For the grounds for dating this work 1139–40, see D. van den Eynde, op. cit., pp. 107–8. The whole group should probably be placed during the years 1131–9.

Ark) that God, as it were, plays with man a game of hide and seek to draw us towards him.[1] The *De Laude Caritatis*[2] is particularly noteworthy as developing the profound connexion between charity and the theology of martyrdom, for the martyrs 'came to their sufferings undaunted, and their flesh despised their outward wounds insofar as love had wounded their hearts within'.[3] For charity makes a wound that it is a delight to suffer, as all the mystics teach. 'Many there are who already bear your arrows sticking in their hearts, and long for them to be driven in deeper.'[4] The deepening of this desire for God is the purpose of the periodical visitations and withdrawals of God's presence, as the *De Amore Sponsi ad Sponsam*[5] explains. 'Sometimes he withdraws himself, sometimes he goes away for a season that, sought in his absence, he may be clasped all the closer when he is there.'[6] Such a visitation is described at the close of the *De Arrha Animae*:

'Suddenly I am renewed and completely changed, and it begins to be well with me, far better than I can say. My conscience rejoices, all the suffering of my past trials is forgotten; my mind exults, my understanding becomes clear, my heart radiant, my desires glad, and at once I seem to be somewhere else, I know not where. I hold something in an inner embrace of love, and know not what it be, save that I would keep it always, and strive with all my might never to lose it. My mind is somehow involved in a delightful struggle not to depart from what it longs to embrace for ever and is supremely, unspeakably exultant, as though it had found in this the end of all its desires, asking nothing more, desiring nothing further, wishing ever to be thus. Can this be my beloved?'[7]

[1] See *Noah's Ark*, Bk. IV, ch. 8 and 9.

[2] MPL, clxxvi, col. 969 ff. English trans. by a Religious of C.S.M.V. *Hugh of St. Victor: The Divine Love* (London, 1956).

[3] MPL, clxxvi, col. 972B.

[4] MPL, clxxvi, col. 975A.

[5] MPL, clxxvi, col. 987 ff. English translation included in the work cited in note (2).

[6] MPL, clxxvi, col. 987B.

[7] MPL, clxxvi, col. 970B.

This visitation comes at the end of a meditation upon the works of God in creation and redemption, conceived as applied to the soul in an entirely personal manner. The presentation is perhaps more concise and complete than in any previous treatise, but it follows the pattern of reflection, meditation and contemplation which runs through all Hugh's major spiritual works. Of that pattern probably the most impressive account occurs early in the unfinished commentary on *Ecclesiastes*,[1] the last work of all. Once again Hugh takes up the image of a fire getting under way. He had already used this in the first treatise on the Ark, but now he makes of it something incomparably finer. With consummate art he describes the beginnings in the green wood, the mounting column of smoke, the blaze that clears and dies back, as the fire gains a complete mastery:

'Since the truth has now been found and charity made perfect, nothing but the one thing is sought; in the pure fire of love, with the utmost peace and joy, the soul is gently beaten back. Then, the whole heart turned into the fire of love, God is truly known to be all in all. For he is received with a love so deep that apart from him nothing is left to the heart, even of itself.'[2]

It is a rare glimpse of Hugh of St. Victor, at the term of his vast endeavour as a *doctor ecstaticus*. In some ways, such a man could have no successor, though he had many sons. His whole life had been spent in the continuous production of works on most of the topics discussed in his period, and written in a variety of literary forms. While he was still alive, his influence was felt all over Europe. Yet his disciples, acknowledging their debt, inevitably made something rather different of the ideas which he had left them. Thus, even in his own house, the work on the pseudo-Denys, which Hugh had inaugurated in his commentary, was to be used by Richard of St. Victor in a far more vital way than Hugh himself had ever used it. The difference between the two men almost marks the difference between one

[1] MPL, clxxv, cols. 116D–118C. The complete passage is translated in the present volume (see p. 00 ff.).

[2] MPL, clxxv, col. 118B. (See p. 183.)

generation of writers and another. In his universality Hugh belonged to the world that also produced St. Bernard of Clairvaux, 'the last of the Fathers'. Richard already seems to belong to the world of the specialist.

NOAH'S ARK: I

(De Arca Noe Morali)

Book I

CHAPTER 1[1]

The author's reason for embarking on this work

When I was one day sitting with the assembled brethren, and replying to the questions which they asked, many matters came up for discussion. Finally the conversation was so directed that we began with one accord to marvel at the instability and restlessness of the human heart, and to sigh over it. And the brethren earnestly entreated that they might be shown the cause of these unstable movements in man's heart, and further particularly begged to be taught if such a serious evil as this could be countered by any skill or by the practice of some discipline. Desiring to satisfy their charity on both these accounts as far as we were able by God's inspiration, we dealt with the main difficulty of these two problems by advancing arguments derived both from reason and from authority.

Knowing, however, that some points in the discussion particularly pleased the brethren, I felt impelled to commit those to writing, not so much because I thought them worthy to be written down as because I knew that some people had not previously heard these ideas, and therefore found them all the more to their liking.

CHAPTER 2

Why the human heart has this disease of instability, and how it may be cured

The thing we have to do, therefore, is first to show whence such great mutability arises in the heart of man, and then to

[1] Chapters 1 and 2 of this translation form the Prologue in MPL, clxxvi, cols. 617–20.

suggest the way in which the human mind can be brought to steady peace, and how it can be kept in that selfsame stability. And, though I doubt not that it is the property of divine grace to bring about this work, and that possession of such grace comes about not so much by man's activity as by the gift of God and the inbreathing of the Holy Spirit, nevertheless I know that God would have us work along with Him, and that He so offers the gifts of His lovingkindness to the thankful that from the thankless He often takes away the very things that formerly He gave.

Moreover, there is a further reason why it is not unprofitable for us to acknowledge both how great our weakness is and by what means it may be remedied; for a man who does not know how great a grace has been conferred on him does not understand how great is the gratitude which he owes to the Bestower.

The first man, then, was made in such a way that, if he had not sinned, the power of contemplation would have kept him always in his Maker's presence. By always seeing Him he would thus always have loved Him, by always loving Him he would always have cleaved to Him, and, by always cleaving to Him who is immortal, he too would have possessed in Him life without end. This was, therefore, the one, true good of man, to wit, the full and perfect knowledge of his Maker—full, you must understand, after that fullness which he received at his creation, not after that which he was to receive hereafter, when his obedience was fulfilled. But he was banished from the face of the Lord when, smitten with the blindness of ignorance through his sin, he came forth from the inward light of contemplation. And the more he forgot the sweetness of supernal things, for which he had already lost the taste, the more did he bend his spirit down to earthly desires.

In this way he became 'a wanderer and a fugitive upon the earth';[1] a wanderer on account of disordered desire, and a fugitive because of guilty conscience, the voice whereof is fittingly suggested by those words, 'whosoever findeth me shall slay

[1] Gen. iv, 14.

me'.[1] For every temptation that assails it overthrows the soul that is bereft of the divine assistance.

Thus, once it had begun to lose its integrity through its earthly desires, the human heart, which had hitherto kept its stability in cleaving to divine love and remained one in the love of the One, was as it were divided into as many channels as there were objects that it craved, once it had begun to flow in different directions through earthly longings. And that is how it happens that the soul, not knowing how to love its true good, is never able to maintain its stability. Failing to find what it longs for in those things which it has, its desire is always reaching out in pursuit of the unattainable; and so it never has rest. Therefore, from movement without stability is born toil without rest, travel without arrival; so that our heart is always restless till such time as it begins to cleave to Him,[2] in whom it may both rejoice that its desire lacks nothing, and be assured that what it loves will last eternally.

See, we have shown you these stages—the disease itself, a wavering heart, unstable and restless; the cause of the disease which is clearly love of the world; and the remedy of the disease which is the love of God. And to these must be added a fourth, namely, the application of the remedy, that is, the way in which we may attain to the love of God. For without this it would be of little or no profit to know all the rest.

CHAPTER 3[3]

Of the difference between the love of God and the love of the world, illustrated by the figure of water changed to wine[4]

The difference between the love of God and the love of the world is this: the love of this world seems at the outset sweet, but has a bitter end; the love of God, by contrast, is bitter to

[1] Ibid.

[2] Cf. St. Augustine, Confessions, i, 1.

[3] Chapters 3 and 4 = MPL, clxxvi, cols. 619–21 (Bk. I, ch. 1).

[4] The Latin of the last phrase is simply *per aquam in vinum mutatum*. MPL, clxxvi, col. 619.

begin with, but is full of sweetness in its end. This, in a most beautiful allegorical sense—for it was uttered of our Bridegroom's wedding—is shown by the Gospel when it says: 'Every man at the beginning doth set forth good wine, and only after men have drunk well that which is inferior; but thou hast kept the good wine until now.'[1] Every man, that is, carnal man, does indeed set forth good wine at the beginning, for he finds a certain spurious sweetness in his pleasure. But once the rage of his evil longing has saturated his mind, then he provides inferior wine to drink, because a sudden pricking of conscience assails his thought, which till now had enjoyed a spurious delight, and grievously torments him. Our Bridegroom, on the other hand, offers the good wine last when He allows the heart, which He intends to fill with the sweetness of His love, first to pass beneath the bitter harrow of afflictions;[2] so that, having tasted bitterness, it may quaff with greater eagerness the most sweet cup of charity. And this is 'the first sign'[3] which Jesus made in His disciples' presence and they believed on Him; for the repentant sinner first begins to trust God's mercy when he feels his heart cheered by the consolation of the Holy Spirit after long weariness of grief.

Let us then see what we can do to attain the love of God, for He will integrate and stabilize our hearts, He will restore our peace and give us ceaseless joy. But nobody can love that which he does not know; and so, if we desire to love God, we must first make it our business to know Him, and this especially since He cannot be known without being loved. For so great is the beauty of His loveliness that no one who sees Him can fail to love Him. A man who wants to make himself acquainted with another person's character and inmost thoughts gets on to friendly terms with him, and is often at his house and in the company of those who are his intimates. And if he perceives this man's affairs to be well and wisely ordered, he at once becomes the more certain of his excellence, and immediately

[1] See John ii, 10.
[2] *Quadam prius tribulationum compunctione amaricari sinit.*
[3] See John ii, 11.

considers him worthy of his love because he knows that he has found such patent proofs of his worth.

Let us likewise, therefore, inquire where God dwells, where His abode may be; let us interrogate His friends concerning Him. If He is wise, if He is faithful, then He merits praise. If He is kind, if He is merciful, if He is humble, then He merits love. He is wise, if He governs His house well. He is faithful, if it is not in Him to deceive those who serve Him. If He freely pardons those who sin, then He is kind. If He is pitiful to persons in affliction, then He is merciful. And He is lowly, if He rules His subjects not by oppressing but by helping them.

CHAPTER 4

Of the three houses of God, and how He lives in each, and what sort of inhabitants they severally have

But maybe you are asking where this house of God is to be sought, and where it may be found. God's house is the whole world; God's house is the Catholic Church; God's house is also every faithful soul. But God inhabits the world in one way, the Church in another, and every faithful soul in yet a third. He is in the world as ruler of His kingdom; He is in the Church as head of the family in His own home; He is in the soul as the bridegroom in the wedding-chamber. The heathen and the unbelievers are all of them in His house—that is, in His kingdom; for through the power of His Godhead He maintains and governs all that He has made. False believers are in His house—that is, in the Church; for He entrusts participation in His mysteries to all whom He has called to faith. But the truly faithful are in His house, or rather I should say they *are* His house, because by dwelling in them through love He owns and rules them.

We are all in His house by our very created condition. We are in His house through the faith whereby He called us. We are in His house through the love whereby He justified us. If you are in the house of God by your origin only, the devil is there too along with you. If you are in the house of God by faith, there is still chaff on your threshing-floor together with the wheat. But if you are in the house of God through love, blessed are you, for not only are you *in* the house of God, but you yourself have begun to *be* His house, to the intent that He who made you may also dwell in you.

This is the abode of health, these are the dwellings of the righteous through which the voice of joy and exultation[1] ever rings, wherein the blessed dwell. Of this, the prophet longed to see the beauty, in it he yearned to dwell, he was on fire with desire for it.[2] If then this dwelling has begun to be in us, let us go in and abide with Him. There, where He 'whose place is in peace'[3] deigns to make His dwelling, we shall find peace and rest. But if it has not yet begun to be in us, then let us build it; for, if we have prepared a place for Him, He will gladly come to us who made us that He might dwell in us, even Jesus Christ our Lord.

CHAPTER 5[4]

Of the two modes of God's indwelling in the heart of man

God dwells in the human heart after two modes—namely, by knowledge and by love. Yet these two are one abiding, for the double reason that everyone who knows Him loves Him, and that nobody can love Him without knowing Him. There seems, however, to be this difference between them, that knowledge erects the structure of faith by its knowing, whereas love like an adorning colour embellishes the building by its virtue. Each is thus seen to be essential to the other, for the building could not be glorious if it had never come to be, nor could it give delight were it not glorious.

[1] Cf. Ps. cxviii, 15.

[2] Cf. Ps. lxxxiv, 2.

[3] Ps. lxxvi, 2. In the A.V. this reads 'In Salem also is His tabernacle'—i.e. at Jerusalem. The Vulgate (Ps. lxxv, 3) follows the LXX, which vocalizes *slm* as *shalôm*, peace.

[4] Chapters 5 to 11 = MPL, clxxvi, cols. 621–5 (Bk. I, ch. 2).

Now, therefore, enter your own inmost heart, and make a dwelling-place for God. Make Him a temple, make Him a house, make Him a pavilion. Make Him an ark of the covenant, make Him an ark of the flood; no matter what you call it, it is all one house of God. In the temple let the creature adore the Creator, in the house let the son revere the Father, in the pavilion let the knight adore the King. Under the covenant, let the disciple listen to the Teacher. In the flood, let him that is shipwrecked beseech Him who guides the helm.

CHAPTER 6

That God is everything to man

God is become everything to you, and God has made everything for you. He has made the dwelling, and is become your refuge. This one is all, and this all is one. It is the house of God, it is the city of the King, it is the body of Christ, it is the bride of the Lamb. It is the heaven, it is the sun, it is the moon, it is the morning star, the daybreak and the evening. It is the trumpet, it is the mountain, and the desert, and the promised land. It is the ship, it is the way across the sea. It is the net, the vine, the field. It is the ark, the barn, the stable, and the manger. It is the beast of burden, and it is the horse. It is the storehouse, the court, the wedding-chamber, the tower, the camp, the battle-front. It is the people, and the kingdom, and the priesthood. It is the flock and the shepherd, the sheep and the pastures. It is paradise, it is the garden, it is the palm, the rose, the lily. It is the fountain and the river; it is the door, it is the dove, it is the raiment, it is the pearl, it is the crown, it is the sceptre, and it is the throne. It is the table and the bread, it is the spouse, the mother, the daughter and the sister.

And, to sum it all up, it was for this, with a view to this, on account of this, that the whole of Scripture was made. For this, the Word was made flesh, God was made humble, man was made sublime.

If you have this, then you have everything. If you have

everything, you have nothing more to look for, and your heart is at rest.

CHAPTER 7

That Noah's ark is the figure of a spiritual building, that corresponds to Christ's whole Person. From the words of Isaiah the prophet

Now the figure of this spiritual building which I am going to present to you is Noah's ark. This your eye shall see outwardly, so that your soul may be fashioned to its likeness inwardly. You will see there certain colours, shapes, and figures which will be pleasant to behold. But you must understand that these are put there, that from them you may learn wisdom, instruction, and virtue, to adorn your soul. And because this ark denotes the Church, and the Church is the body of Christ, to make the illustration clearer for you I have depicted Christ's whole Person, the Head with the members, in a form that you can see;[1] so that, when you have seen the whole, you will be able the more easily to understand what will be said hereafter with reference to the parts. And I want to represent this Person to you in such wise as Isaiah testifies that he beheld Him. So I shall quote Isaiah's words to you, and from them take the thing I want to show you; so that what the literal sense says, the prophecy may confirm.

Now what he says is this: 'I saw the Lord sitting upon a throne, high and lifted up.'[2] It is high, because it is located in the height. It is lifted up, because from the depths it has been translated to the heights.

CHAPTER 8

What is denoted by the throne high and lifted up, and what the temple is, that is filled

Angelic spirits are, therefore, the 'high' throne, and the souls of the saints, who from this world's abyss have been translated

[1] If Hugh drew this picture, it has unfortunately not survived.
[2] Isa. vi, 1.

to the joys of peace on high, are the throne 'lifted up'. God is represented as 'sitting on a throne high and lifted up', because He rules over both.

That which is said a little further on, however, 'the whole earth is full of His glory', means that every corporeal creature on earth is full of the glory of God. For as the divine essence by means of knowledge guides a spiritual creature, so does it fill that which is corporeal by ordering and ruling it. So, as it is said elsewhere, 'I fill heaven and earth',[1] and again, 'the heaven is My throne, and the earth is My footstool',[2] so in this place we have first, 'I saw the Lord sitting upon a throne high and lifted up', and then 'the whole earth is full of His glory', and 'the things that were beneath it filled the temple'.[3] 'The temple' is the power of understanding, whether of angels or of men, which temple is filled by the things that are beneath it. For the works of God so far transcend assessment that no creature has the power to understand them perfectly. The contemplation of them fills our heart, but our heart cannot compass their immensity. How, then, shall we comprehend the Maker of the works, when we cannot fully take in the works of the Maker?

We may say also that this throne high and lifted up, whereon God sits, is the eternity of the Godhead; for it is said of Him alone that He 'inhabiteth eternity',[4] not because God is one thing and His eternity another, but because a throne implies a ruler. He therefore is rightly represented as sitting upon the throne of eternity since, as there is neither beginning nor end to His being, so is there none either to His omnipotence. He always was, He always was omnipotent. Full ever in Himself and of Himself, He was at once perfect, and yet never overflowed. Well then may the prophet say, 'I saw the Lord sitting

[1] See Jer. xxiii, 24.

[2] Isa. lxvi, 1.

[3] Isa. vi, 3 and 1. The Hebrew text of v. 1 says that 'His train filled the temple', 'train' meaning 'skirts'. The LXX reads, 'the temple was filled with His glory'. The Vulgate, which Hugh here quotes, has *ea quae sub ipso erant implebant templum*, the antecedent of *ipso* being *thronum*.

[4] Isa. lvii, 15.

upon a throne, high and lifted up', for the might of the Godhead at once precedes all creatures in eternity, surpasses them in excellence, and orders them by power.

Next come the words, 'and the things that were beneath it filled the temple'. The temple may here be understood as meaning the cycle of the ages and revolutions of the centuries. For as the ages in their course return upon themselves,[1] they seem by their cycles to mark out as it were the enclosure of a temple, 'the things that were beneath it filled the temple', is to be taken, therefore, as meaning that all the periods of time are full of the works of God, and that every generation tells of His wonderful acts. Or else it may be taken thus: 'the things that were beneath it filled the temple'—that is, the things that filled the temple were beneath it, because whatever belongs to time is found below eternity. For the vastness of eternity includes below itself the narrow paths of time, in that it is both before time, since it has no beginning, and after time, in that it knows no end. It is above time too, for it admits no change.

CHAPTER 9

The meaning of the two seraphim, and why God is said to sit, and they to stand

'Above it stood the seraphim.'[2] The two seraphim are the two covenants. And 'seraphim', which means 'burning', beautifully signifies Holy Scripture, which causes those whom it has first enlightened by knowledge afterwards to burn mightily with love. For when it shows our heart what it should desire, it first enlightens it, and then makes it burn. It burns, therefore, because it causes burning, as it is said elsewhere to shine because it enlightens. For of this Peter the apostle says, 'We have a more sure word of prophecy; whereunto ye do well that ye take heed, as unto a light that shineth in a dark place, until

[1] For this conception in general, cf. M. Eliade, *Le mythe de l'éternel retour*, Paris, 1952.

[2] Isa. vi, 2.

the day dawn, and the day star arise in your hearts'.[1] And perhaps it is in pursuance of this allegorical sense, whereby the effect it produces in the hearts of its hearers is wont to be attributed to the Scripture itself, that it is said: 'Above it *stood* the seraphim.' For it rises when it rouses us up, it walks when it makes us progress, and it stands when it confirms us in our good resolve.

We must inquire, however, why God is said to sit upon the throne, while the seraphim are represented not as sitting on, but as standing above it. And because in what has gone before we have given two interpretations of this throne, we must make this explanation fit them both. If, then, we take the throne of God as meaning spiritual creatures, God is rightly described as sitting upon it; for, that it may be above all things, the excellency of the Godhead neither advances in virtue nor grows in wisdom, since Fullness cannot be increased, nor can Eternity be changed. But whenever the human mind, enlightened by the knowledge of Holy Scripture, is raised to the contemplation of heavenly things, it does indeed mount the throne, if it also climbs above the choirs of angels and attains to the presence of its Creator. Once there, however, it does not sit, it stands. For it has come by toil to a point at which it has no natural power to stay. Thus standing is the posture of one who works, sitting of Him who rests. And so we stand on the throne and God sits on it, for we are by grace beginning to be where He is by nature.

In the same way, if we take the throne as meaning God's eternity, we understand ourselves as standing on it, because we can attain His immortality only by passing through the toil of death; it is by adoption that we, who are by nature subject to this latter end, are made heirs of eternity.[2]

[1] 2 Pet. i, 19.
[2] See e.g. Rom. viii, 15–17; Gal. iv, 3–7; Eph. i, 3–14.

CHAPTER 10

The meaning of the seraphim's two pairs of wings, and of the fact that the Lord's head and feet are covered, not His body

'The one had six wings, and the other had six wings.'[1] That is to say, each seraph had six wings, joined two and two to make three pairs. Each covers his own body, not the Lord's, with two wings; that is the first pair. Each spreads out two, the one to cover not his own head, but the Lord's, the other to cover not his own feet, but the Lord's; that makes the second pair. Each flies with two, the one beating against the other; that makes the third pair.

If, then, the seraphim denote Holy Scripture, the three pairs of wings are the three senses of this selfsame Scripture, history, allegory, and tropology,[2] each of which is therefore twofold, since it enkindles the souls of those who read with the love of God and of their neighbour. The two wings which cover the body of the seraph are the historical sense, which covers mystical meanings beneath the veil of the letter. The two wings which are extended to cover the head and the feet of the Lord are the allegorical sense. For when we learn the mysteries of Holy Scripture, we come by the illumination of our minds to the knowledge of His Godhead who is before all things and after all things.

One must understand, however, that though the extended wings reach to the head and feet, they cover while they touch. For whenever we are caught up into ecstasy of soul to ponder His eternity, we find in Him no beginning and no end. For we reach to His head, when we reflect that He was before all things; yet with this same wing we veil His head, since we cannot understand how it is that in Him there is neither beginning nor end. We reach out to His feet, when we consider that, not in time but in eternity, He is after all things; yet we

[1] Vulg. Isa. vi, 2; cf. A.V. loc. cit.

[2] Cf. pp. 23 ff; and for a discussion of Hugh's use of the senses of Scripture, see B. Smalley, *The Study of the Bible in the Middle Ages*, 2nd ed., pp. 88 ff.

cover His feet when we find in Him no end. So by touching His head we touch His feet also; for the more the human spirit strives to search out His eternity, the more does it marvel at His surpassing of all understanding.

That which is written in Isaiah, however, is not 'they covered His head', but 'they covered His face'.[1] And this must be understood in the same sense as that which was said to Moses: 'Thou canst not see My face: for there shall no man see Me, and live.'[2] The full knowledge of the Godhead, which is promised to the saints in the life everlasting, and of which the apostle says, we shall see Him 'face to face', and again, 'Then shall I know, even as also I am known',[3] is veiled and hidden from those still living in this mortal state. But in that everlasting life it is not veiled, but unveiled and made clear, as the Lord bears witness with reference to the angels in the gospel, saying, 'Their angels do always behold the face of the Father'.[4]

Since therefore for our present purposes it is more suitable that the face should remain exposed, in order that the truth may be verified that we cannot understand any beginning in God, we pass over rather than change the words of the prophet, and veil the head from above. And in order that those other words may stand, 'their angels do always behold the face of the Father in heaven', we leave the face uncovered. Other things also, which are here said otherwise, must be taken in conjunction not with the prophecy but with the picture.

'With twain they did fly.'[5] Those two wings with which the seraphim flew denote the tropological sense. For when through reading Holy Scripture we are prepared for doing good works, we are lifted up to higher things, as it were on wings. We fly with them, moreover, one against another, when we encourage each other by the pursuit of well-doing. And we cry 'Holy, Holy, Holy'[6] as we fly, if through our good works we seek not our own greater glory, but that of our Father who is in heaven. For what does crying 'Holy, Holy, Holy' mean, if not proclaiming the glory of our Maker which we have known within?

[1] Isa. vi, 2. [2] Exod. xxxiii, 20. [3] See 1 Cor. xiii, 12.
[4] Matt. xviii, 10. [5] Isa. vi, 2. [6] See Isa. vi, 3.

Having thus briefly explained these matters, let us now begin to treat of those that follow. For now that we have shown the meaning of that which we read, to the effect that the Lord's head and feet are hidden from us, it remains to show what should be thought concerning the remainder of His body.

If then we have taught you that the head of God is that which was before the foundation of the world, and His feet that which is to be after the consummation of the age, we must take the intervening portion of His body to be the period of time between beginning and end. The head and the feet are covered, therefore, because we cannot discover either the first things or the last. The body is visible, because we see the intermediate things that happen in the present age. This body is the Church, which began when the world began, and will last till the end of the age.[1] This is the ark, of which we have set out to speak; and it reaches from the head to the feet, because through successive generations Holy Church reaches from the beginning to the end.

You must however understand that, just as a human person is subject to bodily conditions, which are not part of his body nor directly related to it, so is it with Christ's body, the Church. She dwells in the midst of a perverted race; and when she is attacked by unbelievers, the ark is buffeted as it were by stormy waves. When however she suffers tribulation from false brethren, the body is racked inwardly, as by noxious humours. Whatever, therefore, is contrary to the well-being of the body, whether from within or from without, is not of the body. But the fact that the arms of the Lord embrace all things on every side means that all things are under His control, and that no man can escape either the reward of His right hand or the punishment of His left.

[1] Compare with this: *Tempus autem longitudinis eius est ab initio mundi usque ad finem, quia sancta ecclesia in fidelibus suis ab initio coepit, et usque ad finem durabit* (*De Arca Noe Mystica*, MPL, clxxvi, col. 685B), a notion which returns to a patristic tradition older than that of Augustine, as for instance, Origen, *In Canticum Canticorum*, Bk. II, *Non enim tu mihi ex adventu salvatoris in carne sponsam dici, aut ecclesiam putes, sed ab initio humani generis et ab ipsa constitutione mundi, imo, ut Paulo duce altius mysterii huius originem repetam, ante etiam constitutionem mundi*, MPG, xiii, col. 134.

Why then should the members of the body worry any more about the well-being of the body, once they know the Head to have such power? He, who in His compassion is aware of the danger and by His power provides the remedy against it, knows what is best for His body. He it is who makes a track across the sea; for, guiding His body the Church through the storms of this life, as it were the ark in the flood, He brings her at last to the haven of eternal rest.

CHAPTER II

A brief description of the four arks, whereof two are visible and two invisible

If, then, we want to be saved, it behoves us to enter this ark. And, as I said before, we must build it within ourselves, so that we can live in it within ourselves. For it is not enough for us to be in it externally, if we have not also learnt how we should live in it within ourselves. In regard to this matter, there are three things that call chiefly for consideration. First, how we must build it in ourselves. Second, how we must enter it within ourselves. Third, how we must live in it within ourselves.

But look what has happened. We set out to talk about one ark, and one thing has so led to another that it seems now we have to speak not of one only, but of four. Of these, the two that are visible were built visibly and outwardly, but the two that are invisible come into being inwardly and invisibly, by an unseen process of construction. The first is that which Noah made, with hatchets and axes, using wood and pitch as his materials.[1] The second is that which Christ made through His preachers, by gathering the nations into a single confession of faith. The third is that which wisdom builds daily in our hearts through continual meditation on the law of God. The fourth is that which mother grace effects in us by joining together many virtues in a single charity.

The first is realized in visible reality, the second in faith, the

[1] See Gen. vi, 14.

third in knowledge, and the fourth in power. Let us call the first Noah's ark, the second the ark of the Church, the third the ark of wisdom, and the fourth the ark of mother grace. Nevertheless there is in a certain sense only one ark everywhere, for there is one only common ground of likeness everywhere, and that which is not different in nature ought not to be different in name. The form is one, though the matter is different, for that which is actualized in the wood is actualized also in the people, and that which is found in the heart is the same as that which is found in charity.

The special subject we have undertaken to discuss, however, is the ark of wisdom. So we shall run briefly through the explanation of the other three, so as to be free thereafter to explain this at greater length.

CHAPTER 12[1]

The visible shape of the ark according to the letter, and certain views respecting its five storeys

Those who want to make a closer study of the truth of what is told us about Noah's ark according to the letter have to search out two things in particular—namely, its shape and its size. Now Origen with reference to the shape says: 'I think myself that, from what is said about it, the ark must have rested on a quadrangular base, of which the corners, as they went up, were drawn together gradually, so that it narrowed at the top to the space of a single cubit.'[2] Many things seem to refute this view; for one thing, this shape does not appear such as would keep afloat. For it is indisputable that so massive a structure, laden with so many and such large animals, and also with provisions, could not possibly keep afloat when the waters came, unless the greater portion of its bulk were at the bottom; this fact we can put to the proof today with ships that carry heavy loads. If, then, as is stated, the ark began to narrow from

[1] Chapters 12 and 13 = MPL, clxxvi, cols. 626–9 (Bk. I, ch. 3).

[2] Origen, *In Genesim Homilia II* (MPG, xii, col. 162).

the bottom upwards, so that the sides sloping towards each other took the swelling billows and did not throw them back, and it was thus not so much the waters that carried the ark as the ark the waters, how was it that the whole thing did not forthwith sink to the bottom?

Another point. When it says, 'The door shalt thou set in the side below',[1] it seems to mean the side *wall*, as distinct from the surface that formed the roof above, in which perhaps the window was located. And again it says that Noah 'opened the roof of the ark';[2] this makes it clear enough that the ark had walls below, over which the roof was placed, immediately above the top storey where the humans dwelt. For these and other reasons it seems to us that this ark must have had walls erected on four sides, over which was set the roof, narrowed at its ridge to the measure of a single cubit. Authority does not tell us what was the height of the walls themselves, but we infer that the walls reached to the base of the fourth storey. For the learned tell us that the door of the ark was between the second storey and the third, in such wise that its threshold was close to the base of the third, but its entrance was cut out above, in the side of the same storey; so that there were two floors below the door and three above it.

And they say that one was appointed to receive the animals' dung, the second for their food supplies, while in the third were the wild animals, in the fourth the tame ones, and in the fifth, which was at the top, the humans and the birds. And it is very likely that, when the ark was afloat, the two lower storeys were pressed down under water; whereas the third, in which were animals that needed fresh air to breathe, was the first to rise above the waters. Thus, for people approaching the ark from the water outside, the door was almost on the water-level.

That perhaps is what is meant when it is said, 'The door shalt thou set in the side below'. Or 'below' may mean that, in whichever storey it was located, the door had to be placed

[1] Gen. vi, 16. The Vulgate punctuates this sentence, *ostium autem arcae pones ex latere; deorsum cenacula et tristega facies in ea*, but Hugh takes *deorsum* with *latere*.

[2] Cf. Gen. viii, 6.

low down, so that the feet of those entering would be on the floor.

If, however, one asks whether or not the height of all the storeys was the same, we for our part cannot judge from authority what should be thought on this point. Nevertheless we ask to be allowed to put forward a suggestion which does not contradict it. For we divide things thus: we allow four cubits of height for the first storey, five for the second, six for the third, seven for the fourth, and eight for the fifth. Thus the height of the walls will be fifteen cubits, and the height of the roof also will be fifteen.

On the outer surface of the walls of this ark little nests or chambers were constructed, and these were fastened to the walls in such wise as to allow entrance to them from without, while on the inside the surface of the wall remained unbroken. And these nests are said to have been made for those animals that cannot live either always in the water or always in the dry, like the otter and the seal. So much for the shape of the ark.

CHAPTER 13

The size of this same ark reckoned according to geometry, together with certain views about three storeys

Of the size of the ark we are told as follows: 'The length shall be three hundred cubits, the breadth fifty cubits, the height thirty cubits.'[1]

There are, however, some who say that these dimensions would not be sufficient to contain so many kinds of animals and foodstuffs to feed them for a whole year. The learned[2] answer these objections on these lines: they say that Moses, who as Scripture testifies concerning him was 'learned in all the wisdom of the Egyptians',[3] put the number of cubits in this place ac-

[1] Gen. vi, 15.

[2] Origen, *In Genesim Homilia II* (MPG, xii, cols. 166–7), quoted with approval by St. Augustine both in *De Civitate Dei*, xv, 27 and in *Questiones in Heptateuchum*, Bk. I, ch. 4 (MPL, xxxiv, col. 549).

[3] Acts vii, 22.

cording to the laws of geometry, an art in which the Egyptians excel; and, according to that, one cubit is reckoned the equivalent of six. Certainly, if this method of reckoning be applied to the dimensions of the ark, it will afford length, breadth, and height fully sufficient to contain enough seed for the renewal of the entire world, and stock from which all living creatures could be bred anew.

It must be understood, moreover, that there was no need for the animals that are generated not by sexual union but from the moisture of the earth, or from dead bodies, or some other corrupting thing, or for those that are born of the union of two different kinds, such as the two sorts of mule,[1] to be included in the ark at all. From these considerations the conclusion emerges that it would not have been impossible for a place of such capacity to contain sufficient stock to renew all living things.[2]

There are some who say that there were only three storeys in the ark, and that of these one was a single chamber, the middle one was divided into two, and the topmost into three. And they say that Scripture calls these divisions in the storeys rooms, but the storeys themselves it calls floors. We have depicted this form in preference to the other, because we were unable to show the height of the walls in a flat drawing.[3] For in this plan the ascending beams are gradually brought together until they meet in the measure of a single cubit.

These things have been spoken about Noah's ark according to the letter.

[1] I.e. *muli*, offspring of ass and mare; and *burdones*, offspring of horse and she-ass.

[2] In this section a passage from MPL, clxxvi, cols. 628C–629D, Si autem . . . declinamus, has been omitted.

[3] This is a new drawing, not the one already mentioned on p. 52.

CHAPTER 14[1]

Of the ark of the Church, and the meaning of its length and breadth and height. Of the three storeys, the cubit, and the hundred years that the ark took to build

It remains for us to see what the ark of the Church may be. And, to put it more exactly, the Church is herself the ark, which her Noah, our Lord Jesus Christ, the Helmsman and the Haven, is guiding through the tempests of this present life, and leading through Himself unto Himself.

The length of three hundred cubits denotes this present age, which extends over three periods—namely, the period of natural law, the period of the written law, and the period of grace through which holy Church is from the world's beginning to its end advancing from this present life towards the future glory. The fifty cubits' breadth denotes all believers everywhere, who are established under one Head, that is Christ. For fifty is seven times seven—that is, forty-nine, the number that means the total sum of all believers—*plus* one, which means Christ, who is the Head of His Church and the goal of our desires. That is why the ark is gathered to one cubit at the top.

The height of thirty cubits denotes the thirty volumes[2] of the Holy Writ—namely, the twenty-two of the Old Testament and the eight of the New, wherein is contained the sum of all the things that God has either done, or else is going to do, for His Church.

The three storeys signify the three ranks of believers that there are in the Church, whereof the first have commerce with the world, albeit lawfully, the second are fleeing from it and forgetting it, and the third already have forgotten it, and they are near to God.

The fact that the ark gets narrower towards the top and wider below means that in holy Church there are more people

[1] Chapters 14 to 18 = MPL, clxxvi, cols. 629–34 (Bk. I, ch. 4).

[2] Cf. *De Sacramentis,* prologue, ch. 7 (MPL,CLXXVI, col. 186) where Hugh explains how he arrives at thirty as the number of books in the Bible.

leading a carnal life than there are persons of a spiritual life, it being always the rule that the more perfect are proportionately few in number. The ark narrows to the measure of a single cubit at the top, because Christ the Head of His Church, who is the Saint of saints, is like to other men in all respects in nature, but in the uniqueness of His virtue He is above them all.

The hundred years that the ark took to build mean the same as a hundred cubits. For the hundred years signify the period of grace: since holy Church, which began with the beginning of the world, received redemption through the immolation of the spotless Lamb[1] in the period of grace. For the ark was fashioned when the Church's sacraments flowed forth in blood and water from the side of Christ, while He was hanging on the cross.[2] When the Lamb was sacrificed, then was the Lamb's Bride born. When Adam slept, then Eve received her form.[3] Our Bridegroom went up to His bridal bed, He slept the sleep of death, He showed forth what availed from the beginning, and did what was done from the beginning.[4] See whether Scripture does not mean to say this very thing, when it speaks of the making of this ark of the Church. What does it say? 'A Lamb', it says, 'slain from the foundation of the world.'[5] What does this mean? It was at the end of an age that the Son of God came in flesh, suffered Himself to be crucified for man's salvation, suffered Himself to be slain, suffered Himself to be offered up in sacrifice. The Lamb was slain, therefore, at the end of the world, and He was slain once. How then can it be right to say that He was slain from the beginning of the world? Could He be slain before He was incarnate? If there was nothing mortal about Him as yet, how then could He die? But if He was slain from the beginning, He was slain before He was incarnate. If He was slain from the beginning, He was slain not

[1] See 1 Pet. i, 19 and Heb. ix, 14.

[2] Cf. St. Augustine, *Contra Faustum Manichaeum*, Bk. XII, ch. 16. (MPL, xlii, col. 263.)

[3] See Gen. ii, 21 ff.

[4] See St. Augustine, *In Joannis Evangelium Tractatus*, cxx, par. 2. (MPL, xxxiv, cols. 1950–1.)

[5] Rev. xiii, 8.

once but often, and indeed always. For that which was from the beginning always was, and that which is from the beginning always is.

But if perhaps you say that He was slain from the beginning —that is, for those who were from the beginning, for the redemption and salvation and reconciliation, namely, of those who were from the beginning, taking what is said about the beginning as referring not to the time of the slaying but to that of the salvation—we shall be doing nothing unbefitting if we say that He was slain both once and also from the beginning. For His death was of benefit before it happened; the promise came first, and afterwards the making manifest. So He was slain from the beginning of the world, because from the beginning of the world people existed for whose salvation He was slain at the end of an age.

Nevertheless when He put on beauty, that is to say, when He took flesh, unspotted, stainless, fair flesh from a virgin body, when He 'girded Himself with strength'[1]—in other words, conquered the powers of the air by His victorious cross[2]—*then* was His seat prepared, *then* was the Church redeemed, *then* was the lost sheep brought back,[3] *then* was the way to heaven's kingdom opened, that formerly was shut.

So now you see why the ark, though it was three hundred cubits long, took not three hundred but only one hundred years to build. It was because the Church, which was from the beginning, was redeemed at the end of an age.

But the fact that the length of the ark is six times its width and ten times its height provides us with an allegorical figure for the human body in which Christ appeared, for it is itself His body. For the length of a body from crown to heel is six times its width from one side to the other, and its height moreover is ten times its thickness through from back to front. So if you measure a recumbent man when he is lying down quite flat, his

[1] See Ps. xciii, 1.

[2] See Eph. ii, 2 and St. Athanasius, *Oratio de Incarnatione Verbi*, iv, 25.

[3] See Luke xv, 4 ff. In the Fathers the lost sheep is frequently interpreted as mankind as a whole, the ninety and nine being the unfallen hosts of angels.

length from head to foot is six times his width across from right to left or left to right, and ten times his thickness from the ground. Six is the number of times that fifty goes into three hundred, and there are six periods in the three ages of the world. Again, three hundred signifies faith in the Trinity, or—because of the letter Tau, of which the numerical value is 300, and which still retains the shape of the cross among the Syrians—it signifies the cross. Fifty denotes the remission of sins, thirty 'the measure of the age of the fullness of Christ'.[1]

CHAPTER 15

Of the five storeys of the ark according to the view of some; of the five states of the Church, and of the peak of the ark

According to the view by which we divide the interior of the ark into five storeys, the ark is the Church, and the five storeys are the five states, three of this present life and two of that which is to come. The first is the state of those who are referred to as carnal, of whom the apostle says, 'I could not speak to you as unto spiritual persons, but as unto carnal, I have given you milk to drink, and not meat'.[2] The second is the state of those who are called sensual,[3] of whom again he says, 'The sensual man receiveth not the things of God'.[4] The third state is that of the spiritual, of whom again he says, 'He that is spiritual judgeth all things, yet he himself is judged of no man'.[5] The fourth state is that of souls who have laid off the body. The fifth state is that of those who rise in soul and body; this is the highest state, and bordering on the highest cubit.

The fact that the walls of the three lower storeys rise vertically one above the other and do not slope inwards towards the topmost cubit, means that, whatever progress we may make

[1] Vulg. Eph. iv, 13; cf. A.V. loc. cit.

[2] See 1 Cor. iii, 1 ff.

[3] Latin *animales*. 'Sensuous' is the Douai rendering. The A.V. and the R.V. have 'natural', Moffatt and the R.S.V. 'unspiritual'.

[4] See 1 Cor. ii, 14.

[5] 1 Cor. v, 15.

in this life, we are nevertheless in some sense still turned away from our Creator's face. For, although we rise by merit, we are still not bent in towards Him by immediate vision.

Hence the Bride in the Song of Songs rightly declares that her Beloved stands 'behind the wall',[1] for so long as we are encompassed with our present corruptible covering we are hindered from seeing His face, as by an intervening wall. But the fourth and fifth storeys are drawn together as they rise; for, now that they have laid aside the burden of the flesh, the souls of the saints rejoice in the sight of their Maker; and, when they once again receive their bodies back immortal and impassible, they will more fully and intimately cleave to Him by immediate vision. For what does the ark's being thus gathered up into one in its roof betoken, if not the fact that, when we have been led forth from the darkness of this present life, we shall then relate the fruition of all our desires to one thing? We shall then have begun to see God as He is, so that we shall desire nothing else save to behold His face unceasingly, to fill ourselves unwearyingly with His sweetness, and fully and unfailingly enjoy His love? *This* is what it is to tend to Him, and to attain to Him, always to seek Him by desire, find Him by knowledge and touch Him by taste.

To the storey that adjoined the bottom was consigned the animals' dung, which is a fit figure for the life of carnal persons; since what but rottenness do they produce who serve the longings of the flesh?

The second storey after that contains the animals' foodstores, which suitably signify those who occupy as it were a middle place in holy Church; in that they neither completely succumb to the forbidden desires of the flesh, nor by despising the world do they quite attain the level of the spiritual. But, since those who gather spiritual things from the spiritual through the dispensation of the word of God give their teachers the support of their worldly substance, what are they but foodstores for the holy animals?

It is true that the third storey contains animals, but these are

[1] See Song of Sol. ii, 9.

wild ones, and by them is indicated the life of spiritual persons, who, as long as they are detained in this corruptible flesh, are at one and the same time subject to the law of God, and yet carry in their flesh the principle by which they contravene that law. Animals therefore they are, since they live by the life of their mind, but wild ones by reason of the forbidden desires of the flesh.

In the fourth storey are the tame animals, for as the apostle says, 'He that is dead is freed from sin',[1] and according to the prophet, 'In that very day his thoughts perish'.[2] For when they issue from the bonds of corruptible flesh, their forbidden desires are tamed.

Man occupies the fifth storey, together with the birds. The vigour of reason and intelligence is denoted by man, and the mobility of incorruptible nature by the birds. When, therefore, 'this corruptible shall have put on incorruption, and this mortal shall have put on immortality',[3] then we, being spiritual in mind and body equally, will after our small measure understand everything through the illumination of our minds, and have power to be everywhere through the lightness of our incorruptible bodies. Our minds will fly by contemplation, our bodies will fly on account of incorruption. We shall perceive with our mind, and in a manner of speaking we shall perceive with our bodies too; for, when our bodily senses are themselves converted into reason, and reason into understanding, then understanding will pass over into God, to whom we shall be united through the one Mediator between God and men, the Lord Jesus Christ.

Further, the fact that the short pyramidal form, which the ark has from above, does not continue to the very peak, may signify that whatever is less than God is less than perfect; for even our Redeemer Himself is less than the Father according to the form of manhood that He has assumed, and He Himself through obedience submits to the Father that which He has not received from Him through the equality of majesty.

[1] Rom. vi, 7. [2] Ps. cxlvi, 4. [3] See 1 Cor. xv, 54.

CHAPTER 16

Of the mystical number of cubits in the height of the several storeys

If, however, anybody wants to investigate the mysteries of the numbers which we have allotted to each storey, he will see the fitness of the number four for the first. For, because the human body is composed of the four elements,[1] and joined together by the combination of the four humours,[2] the life of carnal persons, who are slaves to the pleasures of the flesh, is rightly designated by the number four.

Next, because of the five senses, the number five aptly represents natural[3] men who, though they are not shamefully dominated by carnal lusts, nevertheless pursue and love things that minister to the delight of their outward senses, since they do not know what spiritual delight means.

The number six suits spiritual persons, because of the perfection of their works.[4]

The number seven, signifying rest, is proper to the souls who rest in hope and in anticipation of the glory of the resurrection.

The number eight, which signifies beatitude, fits those who, having already received back their bodies, rejoice in blessed immortality.

CHAPTER 17

Once more, the view of certain persons as to three storeys in the ark, and of the three wills that are in a man

There is still something else that we can say about the first three storeys; for each of us has in himself three wills, whereof the first is carnal, the second natural, and the third spiritual. The carnal will wants to give free rein to concupiscence and un-

[1] I.e. earth, air, fire and water.

[2] I.e. blood, phlegm, choler and melancholy.

[3] See p. 67, n. 3.

[4] A reference to the six 'days' of creation, as that which follows is to the ensuing Sabbath. See Gen. i, 3 ff. and ii, 2–3.

hesitating obedience to the desires of the flesh; it wishes to be subject to no law, to fear no one, and to do exactly what it likes. The eager desire of the spirit, on the other hand, is just the opposite; it so longs to cleave with its whole self to spiritual interests that it wants to dispense with bodily necessity. So between these two desires of the soul the natural will takes a middle course; it neither gives itself to the shameful deeds of the vices, nor does it submit to the trials of the virtues. Thus in seeking to moderate the bodily passions it is never prepared to endure those essential mortifications without which the desires of the spirit cannot be possessed. It wants to obtain the gift of chastity without disciplining or chastising the flesh, to acquire purity without the toil of vigils, and to exhibit Christ's humility without throwing worldly honour overboard. And finally it wants to pursue the benefits of the future, without losing those of the present.

Such a will would never lead us to true perfection, but would establish us in a deplorable state did not invading forces disrupt this most lukewarm interior condition. For when we follow this will and we want to relax a little, at once the stings of the flesh arise and they will certainly not allow us to remain in that hurtful purity of lukewarmness in which we take pleasure, but they drag us towards that way, frightening and full of the briars of vices, of which we stand in dread.

And again, when we are inflamed with spiritual fervour, we want to put down the works of the flesh without any regard to human frailty, and in the pride of our hearts would give our whole selves over to immoderate religious practices. But the weakness of the flesh intervenes to recall and restrain us from that blameworthy spiritual excess, and to reduce the pace. And so when each of these desires opposes the other in this conflict, it brings about a state in which the natural will, not wanting either to give itself wholly to carnal desires, nor to toil at the labours of the virtues, is tempered by just control. A certain equilibrium is established by balancing the spirit against the flesh in the scales of our body, and this prevents a preponderance either of the soul aflame with spiritual fervour on the one hand, or of the flesh with the stings of the vices on the other. This makes that lukewarm condition of our natural will impossible. For our soul's health we are compelled to come to that fourth condition which we do not desire, wherein we acquire the virtues not by idleness and ease, but by continual sweat and compunction of spirit; lest, if we remain in that thoroughly pernicious tepidity, God should begin to spew us out of His mouth.[1]

It is of this conflict between flesh and spirit and of the fruit thereof that the apostle shows us when he says: 'This I say then, Walk in the spirit, and ye shall not fulfil the lust of the flesh. For the flesh lusteth against the spirit, and the spirit against the flesh: and these are contrary the one to the other: so that whatsoever things ye would not, those ye do.'[2]

CHAPTER 18

The tropological significance of the dimensions of the ark

But to speak now in terms of tropology, whoever makes it his endeavour to cut himself off from the enjoyment of this world and cultivate the virtues, must with the assistance of God's grace erect within himself a building of virtues three hundred cubits long in faith of Holy Trinity, fifty cubits wide in charity, and thirty cubits high in the hope that is in Christ, a building long in good works and wide in love and lofty in desire, so that his heart may be where Christ is seated at the right hand of God.[3] Wherefore He also had His head placed high upon the cross when He was crucified, but His hands were stretched across its width, that our hearts' love might reach even to include our enemies. The body of the Crucified was placed lengthways upon the cross, that our actions may be not half-hearted but fervent and persistent to the end.

[1] See Rev. iii, 14–16.
[2] Vulg. Gal. v, 17; cf. A.V. loc. cit.
[3] See e.g. Col. iii, 1.

Book II

CHAPTER I[1]

Of what material the ark of wisdom must be made, and how it is covered with pitch inside and out

We must distinguish what we are now about to say about the ark of wisdom from those things which, according to the allegorical sense, we have already applied to the Church in the foregoing book. What we showed there in the sphere of existence is here being investigated in the sphere of thought. For things have their own kind of being in the mind of man, where even those which, in themselves, are past can coexist with those yet to come. And in this respect the rational soul bears a certain resemblance to its Maker. For as in the mind of God the causes of all things exist eternally without change or temporal differentiation, so also in our minds things past, things present, and things future exist together by the means of thought.

If, then, we have begun to live persistently in our own heart through the practice of meditation, we have already in a manner ceased to belong to time; and, having become dead as it were to the world, we are living inwardly with God. We shall then easily make light of anything that fortune brings upon us outwardly, if our heart is there fixed where we are not subject to change, where we neither seek to have again things past, nor look for those to come, where we neither desire the pleasant things of this life, nor fear things contrary.

Let us therefore have right thoughts, let us have pure and profitable thoughts, for of such material we shall build our ark. These are the timbers that float when they are put into the water and burn when placed in the fire; for the tide of fleshly pleasures does not weigh down such thoughts, but the flame of

[1] Chapters 1 and 2 = MPL, clxxvi, cols. 635–6 (Bk. II, ch. 1).

charity enkindles them. Nor should you fear to have this fire in your house—rather, woe betide you if your dwelling is not aflame with it.

Next, you will cover your ark with pitch inside and out—outside, so that you may show gentleness, and inside, that you lose not charity. For by no means whatsoever will you be able to rest in comfort in your inmost conscience, unless you have first learnt through gentleness to bear with evil persons outwardly, and by means of charity have learnt how not to hate them inwardly. Pitch is of a fiery nature, and is born of earth that has been struck by lightning; and charity is generated in the soul stricken with fear of divine judgement.

CHAPTER 2

The meaning of the length and breadth and height in the ark of wisdom

Next let us consider the measurements of the ark, and how they may be realized in us. We said just now that three hundred cubits denotes this present age.[1] If, then, you have made your thought to range from the world's beginning to its end, and have considered as you went what marvels, what great marvels God has wrought and is still working for His elect, and through them, and by means of them, then you have made the lengthways measure of your heart three hundred cubits. Again, if you review the Church in thought and, having contemplated the believers' way of life, adopt it as your pattern, you stretch your heart to fifty cubits wide. And if you have acquired the science of the Holy Writ, which is comprised in thirty books,[2] you build your heart up to the height of thirty cubits.

This is the ark that you must build. These are the bounds of your fathers, which it is not lawful for you to pass, which the Most High appointed according to the number of the children of Israel when He separated the sons of Adam and divided the nations.[3] This is the land in which you ought to dwell and feed upon its riches. Rest, then, within these walls, abide under this

[1] See p. 64. [2] See p. 64, n. 2. [3] Deut. xxxii, 8.

roof, dwell in this house. Storm and tempest rage outside, if you issue forth in any direction at all you will be wrecked. If in your pride you try to use your wisdom to pry into such mysteries of God as He has not intended to open to us through His Scripture, then you exceed the height of thirty cubits. If you do not believe that the Church will continue till the end of the age, but think that God at some time must abandon it, then you go beyond the three hundred cubits' length. If it is your pleasure frequently to think of those who love the world and of their empty conversation, then you transgress the measure of the fifty cubits' width.

CHAPTER 3[1]

The meaning of the door and window of the ark, and why the one is below and the other above

As we have said before, the ark of the flood is the secret place of our own heart, in which we must hide from the tumult of this world. But because the feebleness of our condition itself prevents our staying long in the silence of inward contemplation, we have a way out by the door and window. The door denotes the way out through action, the window the way out through thought. The door is below, the window above, because actions pertain to the body and thoughts to the soul. That is why the birds went out through the window and the beasts and men through the door. And that the bird denotes the soul and the man the body we know from the Book of Job, where it is said, 'Man is born for labour, and the bird for flight'.[2] For we are so born in this life that, if we desire to uplift our souls through contemplation, we must first wear down our bodies by the discipline of work. But the fact that the door is situated in the side denotes that we must never leave the secret chamber of our heart through our own deliberate choice, but only as necessity may happen to demand. And perhaps it is not without

[1] Chapter 3 = MPL, clxxvi, cols. 636–7 (Bk. II, ch. 2).
[2] Vulg. Job v, 7; cf. A.V. loc. cit.

reason that Scripture says nothing about this in regard to the window; for, although it is sometimes permissible to issue forth through thought, yet we must never go outside through work, save of necessity.

This same thing is moreover fittingly conveyed by the fact that the man himself opened the window when he would, in order to send out the bird; but we read about the door that it was both shut from without by God, and reopened by Him, that the man might issue forth.[1]

CHAPTER 4[2]

Of the four ways of going out through action

Now we go out by action in four ways. For some actions are carnal—those, that is to say, which are concerned with physical need; others are spiritual, and are concerned with the instruction of the mind. Good men and bad go forth for both. Those who are enslaved to the outward fulfilling of their lusts are like the unclean animals that went forth from the ark. Those, however, who discharge them from necessity are animals indeed, but clean. But some are given positions of authority in the Church, and to fulfil these is of course a spiritual occupation. So they do not come out from their secret place of inward quiet into public life from ambition, but as a matter of obedience; they are like Noah, who on leaving the ark offered a sacrifice.[3] For the heavier the losses of interior quiet that such persons know themselves to have sustained, so much the more do they frequently do to death by abstinence all the fleshly impulses within themselves. But those who receive honours in the Church for their own glory, and look down on others when they see themselves set high, will not from compassion condescend to weaker brethren in the Church. Such men are like Ham, who made

[1] See Gen. viii, 6; vii, 16; viii, 15 ff.

[2] Chapter 4 = MPL, clxxvi, col. 637 (Bk. II, ch. 3).

[3] Gen. viii, 18 ff.

mock of his father's nakedness, thus bringing down a curse upon himself.[1]

CHAPTER 5[2]

Of the four ways of going out through contemplation, in the third of which we treat of the three voices of the world, and of the raven that did not return

Through contemplation also we go out in four ways. The first way is when we consider what everything created is in itself, and find all things are vanity because, just as each creature comes into being out of nothing, so too its daily changes show that of itself it also tends to nothing.

The second way is when we consider what the same creature is according to the gift of God, and perceive in it the likeness of His mind. For the selfsame creatures which through the state in which they are created are subject to change, nevertheless receive this boon from their Creator, that they never entirely cease to be. Thus after a fashion the temporal work mirrors the immutability of the eternal Author of the work.

The third way is when we consider how God uses the ministry of things created to fulfil His judgements, whether of His mercy in bestowing benefits, or in dispensing sufferings for our merit's sake. By these considerations we discover that all things are the instrument of the divine economy, and the very proof of our depravity. In this kind of contemplation we hear every creature saying three things to us. First it says, 'Receive', then it says, 'Give', thirdly it says 'Flee'. *Receive* the blessing, *render* the debt, *flee* the punishment. The first is the voice of a servant, the second of an adviser, the third of one who threatens.

The servant's voice: The sky says, 'I afford you light by day that you may be awake, darkness by night that you may rest. For your pleasure I bring about the welcome changes of the

[1] Gen. ix, 20–5.

[2] Chapters 5 and 6 to end of par. 1 on p. 79 = MPL, clxxvi, cols. 637–8 (Bk. II, ch. 4).

seasons, the gentle warmth of spring, the heat of summer, the ripeness of autumn, and the cold of winter. I make the days and nights different by a regular progression of variable lengthenings, so that change may take away your growing boredom and order afford you delight.'

Air says, 'I afford you the breath by which you live, and send you every kind of bird for your enjoyment.'

Water says, 'I give you drink. I wash away your dirt. I water your dry places, and provide you with a diet of every kind of fish.'

Earth says, 'I carry you. I feed you. I strengthen you with bread, I gladden you with wine, I delight you with all kinds of fruit, I load your tables with different meats.'

The warning voice: The world says, 'See, man, how much He loved you, who for your sake made me. I serve you, for I was created for your sake, that you in turn might serve Him who made both me and you, me for your sake and you for His own. If you appreciate this benefit, then pay your debt. You receive the favour, give your love in return. This is what He gives, and this is what He requires.'

The threatening voice: Fire says, 'You will be burnt by me.'

Water says, 'You will be drowned by me.'

Earth says, 'You will be sucked up by me.'

Hell says, 'You will be swallowed down by me.'

For as every created thing is of its nature for the service of man, so also does it threaten sinners with the reminder of their evil desert; to the intent that they may fear lest it should happen to them through each created thing even as they know they have deserved. For which reason also it is said that 'The wicked flee when no man pursueth',[1] for the wicked man is just as fearful when things go well, as the righteous man is calm when things go badly.

The fourth way of contemplation is when we look at things created in the light of the use that man can make of them in order to satisfy the lust of his fleshly concupiscence, and consider them not as an aid to our natural weakness, but as afford-

[1] Prov. xxviii, 1.

ing satisfaction to our passions. It was from this point of view that Eve 'saw that the tree was pleasant to the eyes, and was good for food, and she took of the fruit thereof, and did eat'.[1] Those who in this way issue forth through thought are like the raven which did not return.[2] For when they find outside what gives them evil pleasure, they never want to come back again to the ark of conscience.

CHAPTER 6

The meaning of the dove and the green olive branch

The other three kinds of contemplation, however, are symbolized by the going forth of the dove who, when she was sent out and found no rest for her foot, returned at evening carrying in her mouth an olive branch in leaf.[3] She went out empty, but she did not return so. For she found outside that which she did not have within, although the thing that she brought in she did not love outside.

[4]The olive branch in leaf denotes a good state of soul. For it often happens that the more holy men gaze upon the works of their Creator, the more do they burgeon with an inward love for Him. For as a result of seeing the mutability of present things they lose their esteem for all that seems fair in this world and, as it were, return carrying the olive branch in their mouth; since they long to see the loveliness of their Creator all the more ardently for having found so little to their liking among things created. The soul is happy to find its food within, since no pleasure keeps it outside; and, having once been a shipwrecked mariner amid the billows of the world, now that it has been led back safely to the ark, its haven, it fairly jumps for joy.

Similarly, in the second kind of contemplation, as often as we learn to marvel at God's unseen power and wisdom in things

[1] Gen. iii, 6.
[2] Gen. viii, 6.
[3] See Gen. viii, 8–11.
[4] From this point to the end of chapter 7 = MPL, clxxvi, col. 639 (Bk. II, ch. 5).

visible, we bring back, as it were, olive branches from the waters to the ark; since in the changeable things exterior to ourselves we acknowledge Him whom we love unchangeably within ourselves.

Again, in the third kind of contemplation, when we pay attention to His judgements without, we are renewed inwardly by His fear and love.

CHAPTER 7

A short recapitulation of the four kinds of contemplation

In the first kind, therefore, our perception of the causes of vanity breeds in us contempt of the world. In the second, the likeness of a rational being generates God's praises. In the third, the instrument of His economy begets His fear and love. In the fourth, the tinder of cupidity enkindles passion.

Let us beware, therefore, of this going out. Let no one be too sure of his own moral sense. Dinah was a virgin within, she was pure within, she was a dove within. But because the dove, being heartless, was seduced, when once it had gone out it altered both its colour and its name. For so is it written: 'Dinah went out to see the women of that land. And when Shechem, the son of Hamor, the prince of that country, saw her, he fell in love with her and took her, and lay with her, forcing the virgin.'[1] That she was forced shows that she did not go out with intent to be corrupted, but, because she went out rashly, she sustained the loss of her chastity, although unwillingly. But that which follows, 'He made her cleave to him',[2] means this: the raven found a piece of carrion, and did not want to go back to the ark any more.

[1] See Vulg. Gen. xxxiv, 1–2; cf. A.V. loc. cit.

[2] Hugh has *conglutinavit eam sibi*. The Vulgate reads *conglutinata est anima eius cum ea*.

CHAPTER 8[1]

The meaning of the three storeys, the cubit, and the pillar set up in the midst of the ark of the understanding, that is to say, of wisdom

The three storeys in the ark of the understanding denote three kinds of thoughts, right, profitable, necessary. If, therefore, I have begun to love to meditate upon the Scriptures, and have always been ready to ponder the virtues of the saints, and the works of God, and whatever else there is that serves to improve my conduct and stimulate my spirit, then I have already begun to be in the first storey of the ark. But if I neglect to imitate the good I know, then I can say that my thought is right, but unprofitable. For it is good that I should think what I do think and know what I know about others, but it profits me nothing if I do not take it to myself as a pattern for living. For another person's virtue is of no profit to me, if I neglect to copy it as far as I am able. 'A treasure hid, and knowledge hid, what profit is in either?'[2] I hide my knowledge, if I do not put into practice the good that I know; and therefore it cannot profit me that, knowing, I feign not to know.

But if I have taken pains not only to know, but also to perform good and profitable actions, and if my heart's preoccupation is to see how by self-control and a right way of living I can make my own the virtues which I love and admire in others, *then* I can say that my thought is profitable, *then* I have gone up to the second storey. My heart is now more at one with itself; in consequence, it does not gad about among vain and profitless things.

There remains the third kind of thought, that when I have begun to do the works of the virtues, I should labour to have the virtues themselves—that is to say, that I should possess within myself the virtue which I show in outward works. Otherwise it will not be much good for me to have performed

[1] Chapter 8 = MPL, clxxvi, cols. 639–40 (Bk. II, ch. 6 and most of 7).
[2] Ecclesiasticus xx, 30.

the works, unless I have also the virtues of the works. If, then, I direct the thought of my heart to this end, that I may strive to show inwardly before the eyes of God whatever good appears in me outwardly to human sight, then I have gone up into the third storey, where the essential virtues are to be found. But among all these there is one that is supremely necessary, namely, charity, which unites us to God; and that is why the ark is gathered into one at the top, that even now we should be thinking of the One, looking for the One, desiring the One, even our Lord Jesus Christ.

So in the first storey there is knowledge, in the second works, in the third virtue, and at the top the reward of virtue, Jesus Christ our Lord. These steps—if you change the order to 'knowledge, discipline, and goodness'—you have in the psalm where it says, 'Teach me goodness, discipline, and knowledge,[1] O Lord Jesus Christ.'

The pillar set up in the middle of the ark to the height of thirty cubits, to which the entire structure leans, and the top whereof measures a single cubit from corner to corner, this is the tree of life which was planted in the midst of paradise, namely, our Lord Jesus Christ, set up in the midst of His Church for all believers alike as the reward of work, the End of the journey, and the victor's crown. He it is who rose from earth and pierced the heavens, who came down to the depths, yet did not leave the heights, who is Himself both above and below, above in His majesty, below in His compassion, above that He may draw our longings thither, below that He may offer us His help. Below He is among us, above He is above us. Below is what He took from us, above is what He sets before us.

[1] Vulg. Ps. cxviii, 66; cf. A.V. Ps. cxix, 66.

CHAPTER 9[1]

Of the four corners of the spiritual ark, from which we go up to the mountain of the Lord; and of the Tree of life and of the Book of life

This is the mountain of the house of the Lord established in the top of the mountain, unto which all nations flow,[2] and go up from the ark's four corners, as from the four quarters of the earth.

Some go up from the heat of the east, others from that of the west; others again from the cold of the east, yet others from that of the west. The heat of the east is spiritual fervour, the heat of the west is fleshly concupiscence. The cold of the east is the swelling of pride, the cold of the west is the blindness of ignorance. Man was created in the heat of the east, for which reason he was also placed in the garden of Eden towards the south-east;[3] but he crossed over to the cold of the east when he gave himself to partnership with him who first said that he would set his seat in the north.[4] Then he fell to the heat of the west, when after his sin he found another law in his members, warring against the law of his mind.[5] Then too he sank to the cold of the west when, smitten by the blindness of ignorance, he began to forget to eat of that heavenly bread.[6]

In the heat of the east is the foundation of a good nature; in the cold of the east is the beginning of guilt. In the heat and the cold of the west are the punishments of body and of soul. In the heat of the east man was created in the height. In the cold of the east man in his pride desired to exalt himself, and so fell to the depths in the heat and the cold of the west. But through

[1] The first paragraph of chapter 9 = the last sentence of Bk. II, ch. 7, MPL, clxxvi, col. 640. The rest of chapter 9, the whole of chapter 10 and the first paragraph of chapter 11 = op. cit. cols. 640–2 (Bk. II, ch. 9).

[2] See Mic. iv, 1.

[3] See Gen. ii, 8. Hugh's phrase is *ad australem orientis*. Heb. *miqqedem* and LXX κατὰ ἀνατολὰς both mean 'eastward', but the Vulgate has *a principio*, 'from the beginning'.

[4] See Isa. xiv, 13.

[5] See Rom. vii, 22 ff.

[6] Cf. Deut. viii, 3 and Matt. iv, 3 ff.

Jesus Christ, the Mediator between God and man, lo, now these come from the east and those from the west, that they may lie down with Abraham and Isaac and Jacob in the kingdom of heaven.[1] Now the cry goes out to the north, that it give up, and to the south, that it keep not back the sons of God.[2] For because Jesus Christ is true God and true Man, He gives us a model in His manhood and, in His divinity, a medicine. By His humiliation in the weakness that He assumes He puts down pride and enlightens blindness. By the power of His majesty He both feeds our souls with unseen food, and by the overshadowing of the Holy Ghost protects our bodies from the heat of the vices.

The same Lord Jesus thus becomes for us both Tree and Book of life, the Tree because He gives us shade and feeds us, the Book because He chides and teaches us. He chides the proud, enlightens the blind, feeds the hungry, gives shade to those oppressed with heat. Let the proud give ear to His reproof and be humbled. Let the blind listen to His teaching with their mind, and be enlightened. Let those inflamed with the fierce fire of vice seek shade to cool them. Let those who hunger and thirst after righteousness[3] come hither quickly, that they may be filled. Let no one excuse himself. Where the wicked are given the chance to amend, and the good the chance to grow, every man will find the cure appropriate to his disease.

Let us go up, therefore, putting all obstacles behind us. Let us go up with joy, for we are going 'into the house of the Lord'.[4] Let us, the tribes of Israel, go up with joy to the feast of our heavenly fatherland, to praise the name of the Lord amid the towers of Jerusalem. Let us lift up our eyes to see the bright paths strewn along the flanks of the eternal mountains and the footpaths that lead upwards to the gates of Jerusalem. There, on the summit, the standard of the cross, shining with rosy light, makes foes afraid and comforts friends. The doors of the city are open, and in its broad places are the voices of them that sing Alleluia. You will see many people going up

[1] Matt. viii, 11.
[2] See Isa. xliii, 6.
[3] See Matt. v, 6.
[4] See Ps. cxxii, 1.

thither, dressed in their best, people out of every kindred and nation and tongue, some resplendent in rose-red garments, others bright in white apparel, others again brilliant in purple-scarlet.[1] Everyone is in festal garb. A vast and uncountable people it is that has been made ready for the Day of the Lord.

Up there is the King Himself, and He invites us. He is down here too, and He helps us. The slothful are roused, the fearful take comfort, the weak are strengthened, the more eager are filled with energy. Of every age, both men and women, and every estate of life, they run from all parts of the world, and go up eagerly with speed and joy to see the King in His beauty.[2] Each and all, they long to appear with gladness on the day of so great a celebration.

CHAPTER 10

Of the four steps of the ascents

Let us speak now about these steps in the ascents, whereby we climb to heaven, that no one whom the promised prize delights may fear the journey's toil. There is fair climbing there indeed, for, though the going is hard, the love that lies beneath alleviates the toil.

The first ascent, then, is made from the cold of the east—that is, from the swelling of pride; for it behoves the sinner, who fell into sin by disobedience, first to be humbled, and then, by obedience, to rise up again.

The second ascent is made from the heat of the west, for the next thing needed is that we should tread our fleshly vices underfoot, so that we walk not after our own desires but mortify our members that are upon the earth, that we serve sin no more.[3]

[1] *Alios in viola sandicina praelucentes.* A traditional colour symbolism goes back to patristic times, e.g. *liliis virginum, rosis martyrum, confessorum viriditate;* Peter Chrysologus, *Sermo*, xcviii (MPL, lii, col. 476B), and appears among Hugh's contemporaries in Honorius Augustodunensis, *Gemma*, I, 162, viz. *Rosae sunt martyres, lilia virgines, violae saeculi contemtores, viridae herbae sapientes* (MPL, clxxii, col. 594).

[2] See Isa. xxxiii, 17.

[3] See Col. iii, 5 and Rom. vi, 6.

The third ascent is from the cold of the west, for when through abstinence and the practice of discipline we have extinguished in ourselves the passions of the flesh, then we shall be free to give ourselves up gladly to meditation, and to the teaching of Divine Scripture, so that by applying ourselves to reading and to meditation the eye of our mind may once more be enlightened, even as the psalmist says: 'Depart from me, ye evil-doers: for I will keep the commandments of my God.'[1]

The fourth ascent is from the heat of the east, when we have gone on from good to better. For by no means can we ever reach perfection, unless we strive unceasingly to grow in the good things we do.

CHAPTER II

How the height of the ark and the pillar of the same height mean Christ, and how He is for us both the Tree and the Book of Life

Now as to the pillar of thirty cubits' height, which we have set up in the middle of the ark. It is of no consequence whether we believe that this pillar thirty cubits in height, which we have set up in the middle of the ark, was actually there or not, so long as we understand that it was a height of that measurement and size from top to bottom. Again, when we said that the height of thirty cubits signified Divine Scripture, and then asserted that the fact of the pillar being thirty cubits high meant Christ, we were not making any contradiction. For the whole Divine Scripture is one Book, and that one Book is Christ, for the whole Divine Scripture speaks of Christ and is fulfilled in Christ. Our purpose in reading Scripture is that, by gaining knowledge of what He did and said and commended, we may be enabled to do what He told us and receive what He has promised. Growing in this way both in the knowledge of the truth and in the merit of virtue, spiritually we strive towards conformity with Him and 'the measure of the age of His fullness'.[2]

[1] Ps. cxix, 115.

[2] See Eph. iv, 13.

This is the reason why, to make our meaning clearer, we have represented the aforesaid pillar in the middle of the ark, and have inscribed 'The Tree of Life' upon the south side, and 'The Book of Life' upon the north. Wherefore also we have put the thirty volumes of the Holy Writ on the same side, according to their order from the bottom up, ten in each storey. For, as we said, the whole Divine Scripture is that one Book, which is the Book of Life. And you must understand that, since Christ abides the one eternal Person in His twofold nature, He can fittingly be called both Tree and Book of Life according to either nature. Yet He becomes specially for us the Book of Life according to the humanity that He has taken, since as man He gives us an example. He is for us the Tree of Life in respect of His divinity, since in virtue of His Godhead He supplies us with a remedy.[1]

A tree bears two things, fruit and leaves. It feeds us with its fruit and shades us with its leaves. In the same way the power of the Godhead is food for the souls of the enlightened and shade for the weak. The Book of Life looks towards the north, since through the Saviour's manhood, light has arisen for them that dwelt in the land of the shadow of death.[2] And the Tree of Life is turned towards the south, that it may feed and sustain the sturdy with the flavour of its sweetness, and hide those who are still feeble beneath the cover of its wings, as in a noonday shadow, lest they should faint in the heat of temptation.[3]

CHAPTER 12

Three Books, three Words, three Trees

Do not think it burdensome if we pursue these things a little further. For we want now to explain their meaning, not as we do when reflecting, when sometimes we are hesitant, and sometimes we see light, according as the concentration of our

[1] This paragraph = MPL, clxxvi, cols. 642–3 (Bk. II, ch. 9).
[2] See Isa. ix, 2.
[3] This paragraph and the first of chapter 12 = op. cit., col. 643 (Bk. II, ch. 10).

thought ranges hither and thither, but in a few simple words, as one does in teaching.

First, there are books and books. For some are books written by God, and others are those that men write. The books that men write are made of the skins of dead animals or some other corruptible material, and, as these last for only a short time, the books themselves grow old and in their own way are reduced to nothing, leaving no vestige of themselves behind. And all who read these books will die some day, and there is no one to be found who lives for ever. These, therefore, being made of dead things by mortal beings who are going to die, cannot bestow enduring life on those who read and love them. They are certainly not worthy to be called books of life, but would be termed more fitly books of death, or of the dead or dying. So, if I can find a book the eternal origin, the deathless being, and the knowledge whereof is life, the writing whereof is indelible, the sight desirable, the teaching easy, the wisdom sweet, the depth unfathomable, a book whereof the words are countless and yet all one Word, this book will be a book of life. We shall see this more quickly when we distinguish it like this.[1]

There are three books. The first is the book that man makes out of something, the second that which God created out of nothing, the third that which God begat from Himself, God of God. The first is the corruptible work of man, the second is the work of God that never ceases to exist, in which visible work is written visibly the invisible wisdom of the Creator. The third is not the work of God, but the Wisdom by which God made all His works, which He did not make but begat, in which from all eternity He had written beforehand all the things that He was going to make according to the purpose of His providence and His predestination. And this is the Book of Life,[2] in which nothing that has once been written will ever be deleted, and all those who are found worthy to read it will live for ever.[3]

[1] This paragraph = op. cit., col. 643 (Bk. II, ch. 11).

[2] See Rev. v.

[3] This paragraph = op. cit., cols. 643–4 (Bk. II, ch. 12).

Again, there are three words. The first is the word of man, which ceases when uttered. The second is the word of God—that is, the work of God which, once created, never ceases to exist, and yet does not persist unchanged. The third is the Word of God, whom He did not create but begat, who knows neither end nor beginning and is subject to no change. And this is the Word of Life.[1]

Again, there are three trees. The first is that material tree which the Lord God brought out of the earth in the beginning, when He planted paradise in the midst thereof. Man was cast out of paradise, in order that he should not touch the fruit of this tree after he had sinned.[2] The second tree is the Lord Jesus Christ who, according to the form of manhood that He has assumed, is planted in the midst of His Church, like the tree of life in the midst of paradise.[3] The third tree is the tree of life which was planted in that invisible paradise, namely the wisdom of God, the fruit whereof is the food of the blessed angels. The second and the third are the one Tree of Life. But man was created for the third, cast out from the first, recalled by the second.[4]

So there is no tree of life except in paradise. It is not to be found outside, there is its place, there it puts down its roots, there it spreads its branches and brings forth its fruit in due season. And I think it is because it was planted by the springs of living waters, by the fountain that arises in the midst of paradise and waters the whole thereof, that its root can never grow dry, nor its branches wilt, nor its leaves wither, but it remains for ever green.

[1] This paragraph = op. cit., col. 644 (Bk. II, ch. 13).

[2] See Gen. iii, 22–4.

[3] See Rev. xxii, 1 ff.

[4] The rest of this chapter and the first paragraph of chapter 13 = MPL, clxxvi, col. 644 (Bk. II, ch. 14).

CHAPTER 13[1]

How the three books and the three words may be compared with one another

You have, then, three books, three words, and three trees; and, if you want to compare them severally with each other, you will see that the lowest is nothing when compared with the middle one, neither is there the same proportion between the middle one and the top one as there is between the lowest and the middle one. For instance, we have just been telling you about the three books, the first which is the work of man, the second which is the work of God, and the third which is not the work of God, but the wisdom of God through which God made all His works. So call them the work of man, the work of God, and the wisdom of God, and let us see what sort of comparison there is between them.

Now when Solomon had surveyed the works of men and pondered them, he spoke thus: 'Vanity of vanities, vanity of vanities; all is vanity. What profit hath a man of all his labour which he taketh under the sun?'[2] So it would not have been enough for him to have said merely 'vanity', had he not made the twofold repetition, 'Vanity of vanities, vanity of vanities; all is vanity.' Very well, then. If, as the psalmist says, 'Every man living is vanity',[3] then the work of a man is rightly called not only vanity, but vanity of vanity. But of the works of God he shows us his opinion a little later when he says: 'I have learnt that all the works which God has made continue for ever; we cannot add anything to, nor take anything away from the things which God has made, that He may be feared. That which He has made, the same continues.'[4] What then shall I say? If I want to compare the works of men with the works of

[1] Chapter 13 from second paragraph = last sentence of MPL, clxxvi, cols 644–55 (Bk. II, ch. 14 and whole of ch. 15 and 16).

[2] Eccles. i, 2 ff.

[3] See Ps. xxxix, 5.

[4] Vulg. Eccles. iii, 14–15; cf. A.V. loc. cit.

God, shall I call a work of man anything, or not? When it is considered in itself, it seems to be something; but, when it is compared, it appears as nothing, because in the comparison it is surpassed beyond all thought. If, however, climbing higher, you compare what He has made to the Maker, you will find the whole extent of time still less, compared with the eternity of Godhead.

So also is it with the word. The word of man is one thing, the word of God is another, the work of God is not God, but another word of God is God. But a work of God, since it is visible, is called an outward word of His, as being that which issues from His mouth. Yet the wisdom of God, in that it is invisible, is called His inward word, as being the conception of the mind. And as an utterance once made ceases forthwith to be, but the sense of it remains, so what God does is varied, but what God is is unchanged. And as the heart's thought is known through the utterance of the voice, so is the wisdom of God manifested in His work. For this work, this lovely work, this work worthy of the Divine Worker, this work that befits the Wise, this work that the Omnipotent alone could do, at one and the same time in its beauty proclaims as with voice the might of its Creator, and speaks His wisdom. This wisdom has made all things so fertile that the whole of it dwells in each of the things that He has made, and the whole in everything, neither more in everything, nor less in each. Thus everything utters no more, and each not less than the whole and each utter the whole of wisdom.

The Word, therefore, speaks the word. But the word that is made is spoken by the Word that makes, the word that passes by the Word that is not subject to change, the word the senses apprehend by the Word the clean of heart perceive, the lovely word by the loveliest of words, the word that delights the eyes of the body by the word that delights the eyes of the heart, the word created by the Word not created but born, not spoken by the lips but sprung from the heart, which does not pass as it is uttered, but remains for ever.

If, therefore, you compare wisdom's work to wisdom itself,

everything transient, when compared with that which knows no change, is less than one second of a single moment in relation to the longest time that you can think of, that falls within the limits of time at all. So is it with the tree.

CHAPTER 14[1]

Of the three paradises, and the tree of life in each

There are three paradises. One is a garden of earth, whose inhabitant was the first, the earthly Adam. The second is a garden of faith, the Church of the saints which the second, the heavenly Adam, Christ, founded, and in which He dwells. The third is heavenly, and that is the kingdom of God, and eternal life, and the land of the living, or rather the living land wherein God dwells.

In the first paradise the tree of life is a material tree. In the second, the tree of life is the Saviour's manhood. In the third, the tree of life is the wisdom of God, the word of the Father, the fount of life, the wellspring of good, and this is in truth the eternal life.

Now let us make comparison between them. Assuredly the tree of life in the earthly paradise could promote only an unfailing bodily life. But the tree of life of the faithful paradise, that is Jesus Christ, promises His own eternal life to those who eat His flesh and drink His blood;[2] yet He Himself, desiring to show how far removed the sacrament is from the power, says, 'it is the spirit that quickeneth; the flesh profiteth nothing',[3] which is as if He said: 'Do not imagine that it is enough for you to receive Me bodily in the sacrament, unless you have learnt to eat Me also in My function as the word of life, enlightening souls, making sinners righteous, and quickening the dead.'

[1] Chapter 14 = MPL, clxxvi, col. 646 (Bk. II, ch. 17).
[2] See John vi, 47–58.
[3] John vi, 63.

CHAPTER 15[1]

Of the fifteen steps by which wisdom arises and grows in the hearts of the saints

This, therefore, is the tree of life indeed, the word of the Father, the wisdom of God in the highest, which in the hearts of the saints, as in an unseen paradise,

is sown in fear,
watered by grace,
dies through grief,
takes root by faith,
buds by devotion,
shoots up through compunction,
grows by longing,
is strengthened by charity,
grows green by hope,
puts out its leaves and spreads its branches through caution,
flowers through discipline,
bears fruit through virtue,
ripens through patience,
is harvested by death,
and
feeds by contemplation.

But as our discourse has gone on rather long, let us now have a little breathing-space, at the same time beseeching the same wisdom of God, that He who scorned not to redeem us by tasting bitter death, would deign to satisfy us with the taste of His own sweetness, to whom be honour and dominion unto the eternal ages of ages. Amen.

[1] Chapter 15 = MPL, clxxvi, col. 646 (Bk. II, ch. 18).

Book III

CHAPTER I[1]

Of the profit of the fear of God, and of the twofold poverty of spirit

We have shown at the end of the preceding book, under the figure of a tree, how wisdom comes to be and grows in us. The stages of its growth, which we previously compressed into a brief summary, we shall now explain fully and in detail.

In the first place, therefore, it has been said of wisdom that it *is sown in fear*. And indeed it is fitting that wisdom should be sown in fear; for 'the fear of the Lord is the beginning of wisdom',[2] and as shoots come from seeds, so is wisdom born from the fear of the Lord. For charity itself is wisdom, since by charity we taste God, and tasting we know Him. As the psalmist says, 'O taste and see how gracious the Lord is!'.[3] But the fear of the Lord attracts charity to us. For in teaching us to fear danger, it makes us love safety. Thus when the soul considers the pains of hell and the torments that await the damned, it is forthwith struck with fear, and, coming to itself, it looks for a way of escape. Immediately with longing it seeks for Him through whom it knows it can avoid its present danger. And when it has found Him, and has embraced Him with loving desire, then that intolerable terror is assuaged by love. Thus charity is indeed born of fear, yet by means of charity fear is brought to nought.

Further, when the fear of the Lord has come to the heart, it makes it poor in spirit. Now poverty of spirit is a twofold thing. For there are material riches, which consist in having this world's goods abundantly, and there are spiritual riches,

[1] Chapter I = MPL, clxxvi, cols. 647–8 (Bk. III, Prologue and ch. I).
[2] Prov. ix, 10; cf. i, 7.
[3] Vulg. Ps. xxxiii, 9; cf. A.V. xxxiv, 8.

which consist in the possession of the virtues. A person having either of these is a rich man in the sight of God. And both the man who longs to abound in the excess of these temporal and transitory goods, and he who, holding a high opinion of himself, boasts because he stands by his own virtue, are debarred from the kingdom of heaven.[1] But when the fear of the Lord comes to the heart, making us face the thought of the stern ordeal that is to be, and of the strictness of the Judge who is to come, it soon destroys all the pleasure of earthly desire and, by giving us a profitable reminder of our weakness, it shows us what a humble view we ought to take of our own selves.

Then the din of earthly longings is hushed and the heart at once is recollected to the repose of inward peace, and by that selfsame calm it is prepared for the reception of heavenly wisdom. For wisdom cannot dwell save in a heart at peace, and this is why those in whom earthly longings are still rampant do not know what wisdom is. For as blessed Job bears witness, 'The sea saith, "Wisdom is not in me" ',[2] for hearts which fleshly attachments disturb cannot know it. But the man who becomes poor thereby finds it when his spirit, being withdrawn from outward things, is gathered to itself, and he is raised up all the stronger for the contemplation of eternal things.

In this way, therefore, the fear of the Lord makes a person poor in spirit, poverty of spirit calms the heart, and peace of heart is the beginning of celestial wisdom.

CHAPTER 2[3]

Of the work of grace in the heart of man

We said in the second place that the tree of wisdom *is watered by grace.* For just as fear is like the seed, so is grace like the moisture which waters the seed that has been cast into the

[1] See Luke xviii, 24.

[2] Hugh here refers to Job xxviii, 12 'Sapientia vero ubi invenitur?' and then 14, 'et mare loquitur, non est mecum'. (Vulg.).

[3] From this point to the end of chapter 15, the chapter divisions are the same as in MPL, clxxvi, cols. 648 ff., though the titles differ.

earth, and makes it germinate. For when a man's mind has been torn away by fear from carnal pleasures with what might be called a certain violence, it must needs begin forthwith to have a foretaste of spiritual joy; lest, if be left wholly a stranger to pleasure, it should, like a dry seed without moisture, be unable to develop the shoot of wisdom. So by the inspiration of God's grace it comes about that, when the soul has been entirely divested of bodily passions and earthly desires, it is thereupon filled with an unaccustomed joy, and knows the bitterness of what it has forsaken all the better for finding what it is tasting now so sweet. This is the grace poured down from above that waters the seed of wisdom which fear has sown in a man's heart. For a desire for inward sweetness draws those hearts that are not fettered by any outward attraction to fleshly concupiscence.

We may say, then, of wisdom that it is sown in fear and watered by grace, since fear cuts out of the soul its attachment to carnal pleasure; and then grace bedews it, purged now and cleansed from its stains, with spiritual joy.

CHAPTER 3

How wholesome and good a thing it is to grieve about the exile of this present life

We said thirdly that the tree of wisdom *dies through grief*. As seeds cannot germinate unless they first decay in the earth, and in a manner die, so neither can we put forth a good shoot, unless by a wholesome and life-giving grief we first die to this world. This grief concerns the exile of our present life, and it is right that, when we receive grace, sorrow should be born. For once we are enlightened by the gift of the grace of God, and are able to some extent to savour the delight of the good things of the spirit, then it is that we really appreciate how evil is our present case. That is why Solomon says, 'He that increaseth knowledge increaseth sorrow'.[1] For those who have never

[1] Eccles. i, 18.

known the joy of spiritual good love the passions of fleshly concupiscence even when they are in affliction; and for this reason grace, by stimulating a man's heart, prepares it, so that he may recognize his exiled state and learn to mourn the evils he endures.

And so it happens that, after the gift of grace has been received, the heart forthwith dissolves in lamentations, feeds on sorrow, delights in tears, and, prompted so intimately, it becomes the more impatient of the present ills it suffers, in proportion as it longs more ardently for the good things to come. Now it no longer merely leaves the world, it flees it; it not only turns its back on it, it hates it. And whereas formerly, compelled by fear, it forsook the things that it unlawfully possessed, now, pricked by wholesome grief, it sorrows even to have to satisfy those needs which the weakness of man's state imposes. And whereas formerly it withdrew itself from the unlawful activities of the world, now, as far as is possible for one still living in this mortal state, it puts all worldly ways clean out of mind.

CHAPTER 4

Of the three kinds of men, and of the steadfastness of faith

We said in the fourth place that the tree of wisdom *is rooted in faith*. There are three kinds of people, those who have no faith, those who are weak in faith, and those who are full of faith. Those who have no faith are they who do not know God, or believe the gospel of Christ, who think there is no life beyond this one that we now have in time. These sink their roots in the earth, for their appetite for things present is in proportion to their ignorance of the eternal goods that are to follow. They strive for earthly things, and look to be happy here, since they believe that after this life they will be nothing. That fool was one of them, who is derided in the Book of Job by Eliphaz. 'I saw the fool firmly rooted,' he says, 'and I cursed his beauty forthwith.'[1] A fool is one who does not know what he was made

[1] Vulg. Job v, 3; cf. A.V. loc. cit.

for, thinks that nothing exists beyond what he can see, does not foresee the evils that await him, and loves these transient and spurious goods as though they were to last for evermore. It seems sometimes, while he is prosperous, that such a one is firmly rooted. But the wise man 'curses his beauty forthwith', because he knows to what evils he will be snatched away, after these ephemeral good things. Of this same fool the psalmist says, 'The fool hath said in his heart, "There is no God".' And then, including his fellows, 'There is', he says, 'no fear of God before their eyes'.[1] For how can they fear God, when they do not believe that God exists?

It is obvious from this that those to whom the fear of God has not come cannot attain to the beginning of wisdom either.

Now let us consider whether those whom we named second be rooted, or where their roots take hold. They seem to have no roots. For the weak in faith are those who have already acquired some conviction of the truth, but, halting between two opinions still, neither completely gainsay nor yet entirely accept that which is said in Holy Writ about the rewards that await the good, or the pains in store for the bad. For they perceive that certain things occur in this world, from which it may be inferred that God exists and has a care for the affairs of men, and that all men's deeds, whether good or evil, will be subject to His judgements. In view of this, therefore, they begin to fear that God is threatening them; and, driven by this fear, they set about to do what He commands and shun what He forbids. And it sometimes happens that, when they have been practised some while in this fear, they no longer only fear God's threats, but even begin with some inclination of heart to desire what He promises.

Yet again, when they see the wicked prospering in this world and perceive much else in life that goes so awry that it seems the world can never be governed by God's providence, the outcome of everything being subject to the chances of fate, then they start to strive for the peace of the wicked, and long

[1] Hugh here conflates Vulg. Pss. xiii, 1 and lii, 1 (A.V. xiv, 1 and liii, 1) with Vulg. Ps. xxxv, 2 (A.V. Ps. xxxvi, 1).

that they too may prosper in this world. In their unspoken thoughts they tell themselves that it is vain to fear the Judgement, that there is nothing in the tales made up by fools about the pains of hell and the torments of the wicked, and that all this is a product, not of truth but of fear; since surely if God really weighed the works of men so strictly, He could have declared the fact by signs so obvious as to leave nobody hereafter in the slightest doubt.

Lastly, so they argue, to abandon the certain for the uncertain and to pursue unseen things concerning which it is given to no man to know whether they be true, or whether men have been deceived into imagining that they are so, is flatly contrary to reason. To do so is to scorn with a vile presumption assured and present benefits, which in the common judgement and opinion of all men are held to be not only good, but even strict necessities for human nature. This is so the more especially since it is clear that God created them solely for man's service, and it therefore does Him no wrong to use the good things He has made for no other purpose than that men *should* use them.

Men like these, who know only how to weigh their faith against the uncertain issues of events, can never be stable. For, as with a certain lightness of mind they easily believe for a time in the word of truth, they equally easily fall away from their belief in the truth in time of trial, since in temptation they are readily persuaded of its falsehood. Hence they were wavering formerly too, even when they seemed to stand.

The prophet described this sort of man in his own person when he said: 'But as for me, my feet were almost gone; my steps had well-nigh slipped. For I was envious at the foolish, when I saw the prosperity of the wicked.'[1] And a little later, 'they say, "How doth God know, and is there knowledge in the Most High? Behold, these are the ungodly, who prosper in the world; they increase in riches".'[2] For they question and they waver, and they are borne along on the currents of their own thoughts, not knowing in what direction their opinion

[1] Ps. lxxiii, 2–3. [2] Ibid. 11–12.

should incline. They cannot believe, and they dare not deny. They hesitate to give assent, and yet they distrust faith.

But those who are full of faith, they have got roots; yet they do not fix them in the world, as do the unbelievers, but through faith and love they are rooted and grounded in God. They are the vineyard of the Lord in Soreq.[1] They are the faithful vine, the righteous vine, which the Good Husbandman Himself has planted, yes and transplanted too, for He 'brought a vine out of Egypt, and cast out the heathen, and planted it'.[2] Of these things the Lord says elsewhere by His prophet, 'I will plant them, and not pluck them up'.[3] For our land and our country is God, in whom we are planted when we cleave to Him with our hearts' devotion, saying with the psalmist, 'But it is good for me to stay close to God, to put my hope in the Lord God'.[4] From this land we shall not be pulled up any more, if we abide in His love to the end.

Of this rooting the Holy Spirit says also by the prophet: 'Whatsoever shall be left of the house of Judah shall take root downward, and bear fruit upward.'[5] For by those that are left of the house of Judah the faithful are denoted; these take root downward, in that every thought of their heart is fixed on inward joys, and they bear fruit upward, since in their heavenly fatherland, which in this life they ever seek by love, they hereafter receive the gifts of life in recompense.

So the faithful both believe and wait for that which the faithless deny, and about which the weak in faith are hesitant. And the faithful flee that which the faithless love and the weak in faith are anxious to acquire. It is in faith, therefore, that wisdom is rooted, because by means of faith the mind is rendered steadfast and the will made strong. But he who is unsure in faith cannot be made perfect either in the fear of God or in

[1] Hugh is here quoting not from the Vulgate but from the Old Latin version of Isa. v, 2, which reads *Et plantavit vineam Sorec*. It would seem to be correct to take *Sorec* as a locative.

[2] Ps. lxxx, 8.

[3] Jer. xxiv, 6; xlii, 10.

[4] Vulg. Ps. lxxii, 28; cf. A.V. Ps. lxxiii, 28.

[5] Vulg. 4 Kings xix, 30; cf. A.V. 2 Kings xix, 30.

His love. For we fear the thing we are not sure about in a different way from that in which we fear the thing that we believe. That which we believe, we really fear; that which we doubt, we generally fail to fear, because through our very doubtfulness we fall into a certain false security. The result is that we now judge that only to be right, which we see will not be incompatible with what we want; so that our deluded mind often thinks that what it would like our fortune to be will actually come to pass.

In order, therefore, that fear should not be insufficient, nor yet the will lukewarm, we need to have a strong, unshaken faith; so that, being rooted in that, we may establish our hold upon the benefits which we received by means of the three things that went before.

CHAPTER 5

Of what devotion is, and its three parts

In the fifth place we said that it (i.e. the tree of wisdom) *germinates by devotion*. Devotion is the ardour of a good will, which shows itself by unmistakable signs the heart is powerless to repress. It has three parts, zeal, compassion, and goodwill. Zeal is when from love of the right a soul, unable to endure a falsehood against the truth, spontaneously takes the role of its defender. Compassion is when we sympathize with other people's troubles. Goodwill is when we accede to the kindnesses that people ask of us with ready will. And the figure is a happy one. For we say that seeds germinate, when nature by some mysterious power bursts the whole thing asunder to let the shoot that hides within come forth. And in no other fashion does goodwill, unable to conceal itself, burst forth with vehemence, so one may say, to put forth good works.

CHAPTER 6

Of the treasure of wisdom and the field of the human heart, of ignorance, and of the cultivation of compunction, which is likened to a conflagration

We said of wisdom sixthly that it *shoots up through compunction.* Here the gospel parable comes to my mind, in which the kingdom of heaven is likened to treasure hidden in a field. The kingdom of heaven is of course eternal life. But Christ is life eternal, Christ is also wisdom, and wisdom is the treasure.[1] And this treasure was hidden in the field of the human heart when man was created in the image and likeness of his Maker.[2] For the heart of man was so created that from it, as from His mirror, the divine wisdom should be reflected back, and that which of itself could not be seen should in His image be made visible.

Great indeed was the honour of man, thus to bear God's image, always to see in himself the face of God, and through contemplation to have Him ever present. But after that first parent, pursuing the forbidden thing and touching what was banned, had thrown away his joy on earth, the dust of sin cast on the heart of man concealed that precious treasure from our sight, and the outspread darkness of ignorance intercepted wisdom's light. And this is what is signified in Solomon's temple, where we read that, after Solomon had completed all the work to build the house of God, and after all things were accomplished for its furnishing, immediately a 'cloud filled the house, so that the priests could not minister'.[3] Solomon means 'peaceful', and denotes Him who is our peace, who reconciled us to God by His own blood.[4] And because the selfsame Jesus Christ our Lord is the wisdom of the Father, Solomon builds the temple for God, since by the wisdom of God the heart of man was made, that in it God might dwell as in a temple. This is the wisdom that built herself a house, for, descending to earth, she

[1] Matt. xiii, 44.
[2] See Gen. i, 26 ff.
[3] See 1 Kings viii, 10–11.
[4] See Col. i, 20–2.

says that her delights are with the sons of men.[1] But this house, when it is built, is filled with a cloud. For man, once created and by his sin falling away from the vision of inward contemplation, has sunk down into the wretched darkness of this present life, in which he cannot worthily serve God, because he is so wrapped around with the darkness of ignorance that for the most part he does not see what it behoves him to do or to avoid.

That treasure, therefore, is hidden in the field of our own heart, which is found when wisdom shoots. And wisdom shoots when truth is manifested; truth is manifested when ignorance is dispelled; ignorance is dispelled when the mind is enlightened; the mind is enlightened when, enkindled by the love of its Creator, it is moved strongly to compunction. In this way compunction enkindles the mind which, thus enkindled, is enlightened and, when it is enlightened, then ignorance is dispelled. And when ignorance is dispelled, then truth is manifested, and when truth is manifested, wisdom shoots, and with the shooting up of wisdom the treasure is found.

This compunction penetrates the soil of our hearts like a sharp stake; like fire it burns up our corruption, and it dispels our darkness like a blaze of light. With it we must dig deep wells in our hearts, casting out all our earthliness, that we may find the hidden treasures and the secret channel of the living waters. Thus did our fathers Abraham, Isaac, and Jacob dig wells,[2] seeking the living water of wisdom. And when in their absence men of another race filled up the wells with earth, they dug them afresh and sought the living waters yet again; and this they did repeatedly. In the same way when by a zeal for compunction our hearts are cleansed of every earthliness, if lurking evil spirits fill them up once more with earth, we also by compunction must dig them afresh and cleanse them yet again.

And it behoves us to go on doing this until we find the living water, and until we discover the precious treasure. But

[1] Prov. viii, 31.

[2] For this and what follows, see Gen. xxi, 15–30; xxvi, 15–33.

when we have found it, we must hide it, for that which is incautiously displayed is quickly lost. A man displays the treasure he has found when he parades the gift of wisdom that he has received. He hides the treasure found who, when he has received the gift of wisdom, glories therein not outwardly before the eyes of men, but inwardly and in the sight of God. It behoves us also to go and sell all that we have and buy that field, for anyone to whom inward joys have been revealed must for the sight of them gladly set at nought all the things that could give him pleasure in this world.

Among these considerations, however, it is important for those who seek wisdom to remember that wisdom must be sought, not for the sake of something else, but for itself. For nothing is superior to wisdom; and consequently he is unworthy of it, who aims at getting something else by means of it, and seeks it not for the sake of possessing it, but that he may treat it like something that can be bought for money. Further, if Christ be wisdom, the man who seeks wisdom for the sake of human praise proves himself to be like Judas, who sold Christ.[1]

Let us then seek the hidden treasures, let us seek wisdom, and let us seek Christ, but not as Judas did who sought for Christ to sell Him, and not that he might have Him for his own. For Judas sought for Jesus, found Him, and held Him; but he did not keep Him, for He sold Him. The holy women, on the other hand, who came with spices to the sepulchre,[2] sought for Christ, and found, and held, and kept Him, because they sought Him not to sell, but to possess.

We may say, then, of wisdom that it is sown through fear and watered by grace, that it dies through grief, takes root by faith, germinates through devotion, and shoots up through compunction. It seems to me that these stages are denoted where it says that Abraham was bidden to go forth from his country, and from his kindred, and from his father's house, and then finally the country that he will be shown is promised him.

[1] See Matt. xxvi, 14 ff.

[2] See Mark xvi, 1; Luke xxiv, 1.

'Get thee out', says the Lord, 'from thy country, and from thy kindred, and from thy father's house, and come into the land that I will show thee.'[1] We, therefore, get us out of our country by fear, and out of our kindred by grace, and out of our father's house by grief; we follow the Lord through faith and devotion, and after that at the sixth stage our promised land is shown us through compunction.

By fear we forsake earthly possessions, by grace and grief we change our disposition, by faith and devotion we establish our souls, and by compunction we find what we desire. We leave our kindred, when we renounce the vices that arise in us and from us. We leave our father's house, when we put the whole world and all that it contains right out of our thought, and fix the whole intention of our souls on things eternal only. In the birth whereby we are born in sin, our father is the devil,[2] since according to our birth we belong to the dominion of him who is the author of sin. His house is this world, for by his perversity he has justly become the prince of this world and of those who love it. But, when we have left our country and our kindred and our father's house, another land is shown us by the Lord. This is when we, being utterly dead to the world, are allowed to catch, as it were from afar, some hint of joys to come. For the soul on whom the Holy Spirit breathes is gladdened with an unaccustomed joy; and, when a mere fragrance so refreshes it, it wonders what the taste itself can be.

CHAPTER 7

Of the excellency of spiritual longing, which is compared to smoke

Next, at the seventh stage, we said that the tree of wisdom *grows by longing*. For just as compunction resembles a flaming fire, so is longing like the smoke that is born of the fire, that goes straight up, and the higher it goes, the wider it spreads until, lost in the heavens, it disappears from view. For when the

[1] See Vulg. Gen. xii, 1; cf. A.V. Gen. xii, 1.
[2] Cf. e.g. John viii, 44; xvi, 11.

blight of sin has been destroyed in the soul by the fire of compunction and a clear flame begins to burn within the heart, the soul is forthwith lifted to a certain eminence of contemplation where, being somehow raised above itself, it sees as from a distance what one may call a land of light and a new country, such as it does not remember ever having seen before, and never thought existed. Beholding this, a man is filled with wonder, and for joy at the light he now has he condemns the darkness of his previous ignorance. Below him, he marvels to see himself where he lay in the depths; above him, he is amazed to see himself being raised up so high. He rejoices that he has escaped already from so much that made him grieve; he grieves because he still falls so far short of what he loves. He strives, therefore, he puts his best foot forward, he climbs up and he grows by longing; and, as a column of smoke spreads wider in proportion as it rises higher, so such a man, as he approaches heavenly things and disperses every cloud of earthly desire, becomes altogether spiritual. At last he becomes invisible to human sight as, refusing ever again to come out in search of earthly and visible things, he glories inwardly in the Lord's hidden face.

CHAPTER 8

Of the powers of charity, and of the eight beatitudes compared with these eight steps

In the eighth place we added that the tree of wisdom *is strengthened by charity*. Charity is like wine. For wine makes those whom it inebriates sprightly, bold, brave, forgetful, and in a certain way insensible. So charity, by cleansing the conscience, puts new spirit into the heart; and then, as through purity of conscience it gains confidence, emboldens it. Hence it grows strong because, as Scripture testifies, he who trusts in the Lord is as strong as a lion.[1] For a pure conscience cannot be overcome by any adverse circumstances. So long as it is inwardly confident

[1] See Prov. xxviii, 1.

that it will always have God's help, it readily despises and conquers whatever outward contradiction it endures. It also induces forgetfulness, because while it draws the whole attention of the soul towards desire for eternal things, it drives from it entirely the memory of all those that pass. It makes the soul insensible, filling the heart to overflowing with inward sweetness; so that it despises whatever outward bitterness it suffers, as though it did not feel it.

Thus charity strengthens wisdom, since it affords the soul both confidence and strength, and further gives it an insuperable constancy by rendering it in a way insensible.

We can, if we will, see the eight beatitudes[1] expressed in these eight steps:

Our saying that the tree of wisdom *is sown through fear* will then correspond to 'Blessed are the poor in spirit: for theirs is the kingdom of heaven'.

Our saying that it *is watered by grace* will answer to 'Blessed are the meek: for they shall inherit the earth'.

Our saying that it *dies through grief* will answer to 'Blessed are they that mourn: for they shall be comforted'.

Our saying that it *takes root by faith* will answer to 'Blessed are they that hunger and thirst after righteousness: for they shall be filled'.

Our saying that it *germinates through devotion* will answer to 'Blessed are the merciful: for they shall obtain mercy'.

Our saying that it *shoots up through compunction* will answer to 'Blessed are the pure in heart: for they shall see God'.

Our saying that it *grows by longing* will answer to 'Blessed are the peacemakers: for they shall be called the children of God'.

Our saying that it is *strengthened by charity* will answer to 'Blessed are they that are persecuted for righteousness' sake: for theirs is the kingdom of heaven'.

[1] See Matt. v, 2–11.

CHAPTER 9

What the hope of future blessings effects in a man's heart

In the ninth place we added that the tree of wisdom *grows green through hope*. The hope of future blessings in the mind is like a sparkling fire fed with kindling wood. For hope is as it were the memory of unseen joys which, hidden in man's heart, warms it inside, and in the winter of this present life will not allow the cold of infidelity to wither it. And as long as this hope lives in our mind, the tree of wisdom never wilts; but, as a tree preserves its foliage unharmed as long as it has moisture and warmth in the right proportions, so the soul cannot wither that is fostered by the warmth of the Holy Spirit descending from above, and watered by the practice of good works from below.

CHAPTER 10

Of the vice of pride and curious inquiry,[1] *the practice of caution,*[2] *the four kinds of evils, the two necessities,*[3] *and the two desires*

Tenthly we went on to say that the tree of wisdom *puts out its leaves and spreads its branches through caution*. There are some in whom wisdom grows up tall, and others in whom it spreads itself out. In contemplative souls, who by their insight enter into the contemplation of heavenly mysteries, it rises to the height. In active people it spreads itself out; for these, in looking after earthly matters, spread out their attention over many things.

There are, however, some who, through the inward peace that has been given them, at first grow much in contemplation; but, when they see their more artless brethren busy with earthly concerns, they despise them as inferior to themselves and,

[1] There is no exact equivalent in English for *curiositas*.

[2] Latin, *circumspectio*.

[3] The word used here is *exactio*, but in the text *necessitas*.

though they themselves are barren of good works, yet they are not afraid to pass judgements on good works in others. In this way those who fail to continue in humility, being severely shaken by the winds of pride, fall from the peak of contemplation and, being thus cast down, they are exposed to sundry errors, and distracted from their peace in various ways.

Clearly the beginning of these errors is that they will not humbly recognize their weakness, but are unthinkingly puffed up over the gift they have received from God. For in the eyes of people who take such an exaggerated view of their own merits, the actions of others are bound to appear vile, nor could it happen that they should presume to judge another's life, were they not first inflated in themselves.

Once this error has gained entrance to the soul, therefore, it spreads its poisons wide and, creeping secretly and mingling itself with all the movements of the soul, it changes its inclinations, destroys its purposes, twists its thoughts, corrupts its desires, and brings to it unnecessary cares. And, because a person once puffed up has learnt to think thus highly of himself, he disdains to bring his own actions before the bar of reason, and the less he thinks there is within himself that merits blame, the readier he is to hunt down someone else. Yet this pride cloaks itself at first under the semblance of good zeal, and it persuades the deluded heart that he who acquiesces in another's fault is no perfect lover of righteousness, and that he undoubtedly so acquiesces, who neglects to rebuke an offender while he can.

Deluded by this error, therefore, the sorely imperceptive soul gives itself over wholly to the vice of curious inquiry. And by degrees, as the disease increases, while at the outset it makes a habit of chasing after other people's faults without restraint, it ultimately reaches a condition in which, with everything it sees, it tries either to misrepresent it openly, or to interpret it unfavourably.

Thus, for instance, if such persons see that some people are a trifle anxious about common needs, they call them covetous. Those whom they see provident they call misers. Those again who are friendly and cheerful towards everyone are, so they say, given to the vice of flattery; and at the same time they believe that those who generally go about with a sad face are eaten up with jealousy. Those whom they see eager and wholly desirous in service they declare to be light-minded and restless. Those whom they find feeble or heavy they accuse of laziness and sloth. They think that the abstemious suffer from the disease of hypocrisy, and that those who yield more to their necessity are giving way to luxury.

And upon this error there ensues a manifold disorder. Indeed an evil and unwholesome curiosity, that does its wicked best to search out someone else's private business, does not leave off suspecting things amiss, although it may find nothing that it can reasonably blame. But, if it does find something reprehensible, its swollen heart is moved thereby not to compassion but to scorn. Scorn then arouses anger, for the soul swollen by the character of pride finds unbearable anything that it endures from one whom it so scorns. Anger then develops into indignation, indignation leads to insult, insult produces hatred, inveterate hatred passes over into envy, and envy begets a weariness of soul which, when established in the heart, destroys it like the moth; and with the strangling of inward joy the conscience wastes away within itself.

Thus the soul becomes a burden to itself; becoming as impossible to move as is a lump of lead, it cannot be uplifted. And he, who formerly was wont to pierce the heavens on the wings of contemplation, borne down as with a heavy weight now falls beneath himself. He stands in terror of the darkness that he suffers inwardly, and would flee from himself, if that were possible. So, abandoning his conscience, he plunges himself into earthly activities, so that being busy he may forget his ills. And because he judges any evil to be less than that which he now suffers inwardly, wretched as he now is, he loves even the hardships of his outward business. And the thirsty soul, since its heart's palate has lost the taste for true sweetness, drinks avidly of the vinegar of fleshly longing. The devil, finding it thus involved in its outward concerns, corrupts it. And, since it now never says 'No' to itself by any exercise of reason, he drags it towards any and every pitfall of error.

But now that we have told you to what great evils pride may cast us down, it is right for us also to think what is the remedy, by means of which the grace of God may mend us. For this antidote is such that it not only restores us to our former wholeness, but also gives us greater strength; it does not only repair that which has been destroyed, but also over and above adds that which formerly we lacked. Wherefore through it all God, the laudable and glorious, the only merciful and kind, who freely gives His gift and freely makes anew what has been lost—and we did not deserve even to receive the gift we lost—God, I say, so restores us that we seem to have fallen not to our destruction, but for our further growth.

For him, therefore, who had increased in wisdom and waxed proud about the height he had attained, it is a good thing that he should be cut off short and grow accustomed to spread out his branches. It is good for him to be compelled for a time to turn outwards, making a break with the contemplative life and taking up the charge of external responsibilities, so that he may learn by experience how difficult it is to be bound by one's duty to look after external affairs, without giving up the desire for the inner life. And, when he has recognized that he is unequal to the duties of the charge that he has undertaken, then he will know what he should have thought about those, whom formerly he so unthinkingly despised when they were in like case. And because the greater the power, the greater the responsibility that generally goes along with it, let duty itself teach him how to be prudent and sensible, and let him not give way to idleness; so that he may brace himself at the prospect of a risk and consider not only what is actually happening, but also what may happen.

Let him not trust too much to fortune when she smiles, or lose his confidence when things go badly; and let it be a matter of indifference to him whether the result that he achieves be good or bad. Let him plan in advance for every contingency, prefer his friends' requirements before his own, and not set a higher value on his own opinion than he ought. Let him love all men, but not trust them all alike. Let him give his seniors the obedience due to them, affection to his peers, and fatherly care to those for whom he is responsible. And thus, by concentrating on the exercise of the different virtues, let him spread out the branches of his wisdom. Then at last will that tree of wisdom, which had begun by growing badly as a bare stem, like a bending reed, be strengthened by continual exercise of the virtues and clad with the foliage of a universal caution. It will lift up its head to the heights once more, all the better now for being stronger, sturdier, more experienced, and the more fair with caution, so that even its very truncation seems to have turned out to its advantage.

But since it is through caution that this same wisdom spreads abroad its branches, let us lay down some common circumstances in which caution comes into play. There are four of these—fear, anxiety, necessity, attraction.

Fear is worry lest we fall into danger.

Anxiety is concern to avoid the unpleasant and to obtain the pleasant.

Necessity is the duty to give, or the need to receive.

Attraction is the desire to enjoy things.

Fear is a burden, anxiety a weight, necessity a restriction, attraction a wound. Thus when farmers want their trees to spread out, they are wont either to put weights on top of them to press them down, or else to tie weights under them to pull them down. Or else they drive in stakes and tie the branches to those, so that they cannot rise, but spread out sideways. Or else again they insert grafts in the bare stem, that these, when they have taken, may cover the tree. Fear, then, is like a weight put on top, anxiety is like a weight hung underneath, necessity is like a stake that tethers, attraction is as it were a graft that on its insertion makes a wound.

Those four are born of the four kinds of evils to which man is subject in this world—namely, the wrath of God, the vanity of the world, the weakness of our human state, and the malice of the devil.

The wrath of God is when we are chastened with afflictions.

The vanity of the world is when, by going beyond the measure of our real need, we fall into self-indulgence.

The weakness of our human state is that we are easily upset when things go badly, and recover only with difficulty our power to act well.

The malice of the devil is when at his instigation we are stimulated to vice.

So the wrath of God weighs us down, the vanity of the world by filling us with needless cares drags us down, the weakness of our human state ties us down with ruthless restrictions, the malice of the devil wounds us by inciting us to unlawful desires.

In all these things, however, God's servant is practised to his profit, and even these evils do him abject service, since by making him suffer they prove, and do not overwhelm him. All those passions, fear, anxiety, and wrong desire, are evil indeed, and the necessity of this present life also is called an evil by the Lord.[1] But God allows these things to dominate the minds of his elect for a time, so that, when they have discovered by experience what wretchedness there is in spurious delights, they may with the more ardour seek these true, eternal ones, that no sadness corrupts. And for their good sometimes they are abandoned and allowed to give in to the passions of the flesh, that they may recognize their weakness and not be self-confident, and may thereafter yield themselves more whole-heartedly to the grace of God, for having learned clearly from their previous fall that it is not by their own strength that they stand.

There is another reason too why it is sometimes good for the servants of God to be tempted, so that the very temptations may practise them and make them more wary; for struggles with the vices are exercises in the virtues. And just as a man learns by falling often how to tread firmly and walk warily, or as the man who has often been wounded in battle is on the look-out for the coming blow, so he who has been frequently deluded by the devil presently perceives his wiles more readily, and over-

[1] See last sentence of Matt. vi, 34 and cf. Job vii, 1.

throws his tricks. And this is how it happens that we see many persons reach the heights of virtue after many crimes, and wreck the devil's onslaughts on them with such vigour, that where he used most often to rejoice in victory, he now appears, not as despoiling them, but as having armed them against himself. This is in truth the deep, mysterious purpose of the Lord, that that very thing should help His chosen to their crown, which the enemy was flattering himself would bring them down and make the victory his.

Now, therefore, if you please, we will consider first how from those same passions occasions for the exercise of virtue arise, and then through those selfsame occasions caution is increased. For the four are fear, anxiety, necessity, and attraction, and from three of them—namely, fear, necessity, and attraction—is born the fourth, namely anxiety. For we take trouble to avoid the thing we fear may happen, trouble to rid ourselves of that which it is a grief to endure, and trouble too to get the thing we want. And so upon the experience of the passion follows the anxiety, and upon the anxiety the effort to do something in practice, and with the practical measures caution is increased. And since on account of the defects of our fallen nature we are prone to be more anxious to obtain a thing that we desire wrongly, or to avoid a thing for which we have a needless fear, it happens that, in the pursuit of bad things, we readily acquire the wariness of caution which we have failed to cultivate in seeking for the good. Often a man who does not fear the death of his soul is terrified at bodily death, and one who does not give a thought to the pains of hell recoils in dread from undergoing temporal punishments. Frequently the person, who has not yet learnt to fear the confusion that sinners will experience before the eyes of God and of the holy angels,[1] is ashamed to be mean in the sight of men. And men take much trouble to avoid these things, which for the servants of God are not only not things to flee from at all, but even—when they are known by their fruits—things to be desired.

In the same way there are many people, oblivious of the

[1] See Matt. xxi–xxiii; Luke xii, 8 ff. and Matt. xxv, *passim*.

hunger of their souls, who yet exert themselves tremendously to obtain food for their bellies. And to fulfil the desire of their flesh men will often suffer many arduous and bitter toils, which they refuse to submit to even for a short time for love of the life eternal. Yet the elect, by contrast, will labour without ceasing and put themselves to pain in order not to fulfil the desires of the flesh. They are men who are not without fear in yielding even to their genuine needs, fearing lest what the weakness of their state requires should lead to self-indulgence.

Carnal men, however, who gladly endure trials in order to fulfil their lusts, wander abroad not only in their deeds, but also in their spirits; and by the many things they learn from their experience they become wiser, as it were because of their very distractions. Of these the Lord says in the gospel, 'the children of this world are in their generation wiser than the children of light'.[1] But when such as these are by God's mercy converted from their error, they give up their base interests; but the prudence that they gained by means of them, that they do not lose, and they become the more provident in well-doing from having given themselves so wholeheartedly to doing what was bad.

It is thus clearly demonstrated that the fact that they seemed to be abandoned for a time was actually for their good. On that account, as we have previously said, there are four things that make demands on caution, namely, fear, anxiety, necessity, and attraction.

Now there are three worldly or carnal fears, the fear of contempt, the fear of punishment, and the fear of death; and each of these begets its own anxiety. Necessity, however, is twofold; there is one necessity in the giving of what is due, and another in the receiving of what is needful. For you say that you 'must' give tribute to Caesar, and in another sense you say that you 'must' give food to your belly. You 'must' give tribute to Caesar, because that is your duty; you 'must' give food to your belly, because it needs to have it. Both Caesar and your belly are your creditors, both the money and the food are tribute.

[1] Luke xvi, 8.

But, if we look more closely at the matter, Caesar does us less of an injury by taking away our money, than our belly does in taking food. For Caesar, by taking our money only once takes away our trouble about it; but the belly by perpetually requiring food never allows us to be without trouble. Caesar by taking our money away may almost be said to relieve us; our belly by accepting food burdens body and soul alike. Caesar by taking our money humbles us through poverty; the belly by receiving food enkindles our inclination to vice through satiety. In brief, I see a man who serves his belly as in all respects more wretched than one who serves Caesar.

Necessity, then, is one thing in the giving of what is due, another in the receiving of one's need. And that which consists in the giving of what is due is met with in many ways. For superiors are bound to provide for their subjects, subjects owe obedience to superiors, equals owe each other brotherly love, the wise owe the foolish instruction, the rich owe alms to the poor. But since without prudence and caution we can neither rightly fulfil what we ought, nor ask for what we need, in what else, as long as we are subject to these necessities, do we need to be educated, besides prudence and caution?

Attraction is the desire to enjoy things. Of desires, some are good and others bad, and the good desires are spiritual, the bad ones carnal. Spiritual desire, like sweet wine, greatly refreshes us; carnal desire, like a sharp and venomous wine, either drives those who drink it mad, or else it kills them. Of the former wine it is said that 'in the hand of the Lord there is a cup filled with undiluted wine',[1] that is, of the wine that 'maketh glad the heart of man'.[2] And in another place, 'The cup of the Lord that inebriateth, how excellent it is!',[3] and many other things are said in Scripture of that wine. But of the other it is said, 'their wine is the poison of dragons, and the cruel venom of asps',[4] because it is extracted from very bitter grapes, and because

[1] Vulg. Ps. lxxiv, 9; cf. A.V. Ps. lxxv, 8.
[2] Ps. civ, 15.
[3] Vulg. Ps. xxii, 5; A.V. Ps. xxiii, 5.
[4] Deut. xxxii, 33.

Babylon proffers it for drink in the golden cup of her fornications, wherefrom all nations are made drunk.[1] Of this wine it is also said in the gospel, 'Every man at first sets forth good wine; and when men have well drunk, then that which is inferior'.[2] But of the other it is said, 'thou hast kept the good wine until now'.[3]

This carnal desire, implanted in the heart like a strange graft, wounds it grievously. And this is the stranger of whom David was told by Nathan that he had come to the rich man, and that, in order to feed him, the rich man, passing over his own hundred sheep, had taken away the poor man's one ewe lamb. For the lust of carnal concupiscence had come to David like a stranger guest, when, walking on the roof of his house, he saw Uriah's wife, Bathsheba, bathing, and fell in love with her. And he then passed over his own hundred sheep and killed the poor man's one ewe lamb, when he left his own many wives and took away Uriah's only wife to satisfy his lust.[4] Therefore strange grafts are inserted into a bare trunk to clothe it, because Almighty God often allows those whom He sees lukewarm in their laziness and, as it were, naked of good works, to be wounded for a season by unlawful longings, so that they may grow devout and cautious. But in what manner these attractions exercise a person, although they be evil, is difficult to realize and harder to explain. He alone knows, who makes it come to pass.

CHAPTER II

Of the value of discipline, which is likened to a flower wherein are three things that are food for thought, hope, beauty, fragrance

The tree of wisdom *flowers through discipline*. There are three things in a flower, hope, beauty, and fragrance; and we find the counterpart of those in good works. For as the flower contains

[1] See Rev. xvii, 1–5; xviii, 2 ff.
[2] Vulg. John ii, 10; cf. A.V. loc. cit.
[3] Ibid.
[4] See 2 Sam. xi, 2–xii, 9.

the promise of the fruit that is to be, so a good work awaits the reward of future recompense; and we hope that those whose works we see to be good are destined for a heavenly reward.

Again, as a flower is beautiful in its form and pleasing in its scent, so a good work gives a bright example when it seems laudable to those who witness it and incites them to do the like. And its fragrance is pleasing when the good report of it reaches those who are far off.

CHAPTER 12

That the fruit of a good work is the virtue of a right intention

The tree of wisdom *bears fruit through virtue.* The fruit of a good work is the hidden virtue of a right intention. For beneath what appears in the flower of a good work as an example, the fruit of virtue lies as it were hidden in the depths of the spirit. Hence anyone empty of virtue who makes the outward show of a good work is like a tree that flowers without bearing fruit.

CHAPTER 13

Of patience, how useful and necessary it is

The tree of wisdom *ripens through patience* and perseverance. Virtue begun is useless, if it be not carried through. So anyone who makes a beginning in virtue forms so to speak a sort of fruit of goodness in himself; but, if he gives up the virtue before the end, his fruit falls untimely, being as it were unripe and not fit to eat.

Patience and perseverance are, therefore, extremely necessary for us, that we may go on steadfastly unto the end in the good course in which by God's grace we have made a fair beginning.

CHAPTER 14

How the fruit of divine wisdom is harvested by death

When the fruit is ripe, then it is plucked, that it may come to the table of the Householder. And once we have reached the limit of our personal perfection, we too are cut off from this life by death, so that we may be taken in to the banquet of the everlasting King. And this is what the bride is speaking of to her Beloved in the song of love, when she says: 'Let my Beloved come into His garden and eat the fruits of His apple-trees.'[1] And in the same place He in turn replies to her: 'I have come into My garden, My sister, My spouse: I have gathered My myrrh with My spices; I have eaten My honeycomb with My honey; I have drunk My wine with My milk.'[2] By death, then, we are harvested, so that like fragrant fruit we may be offered at the nuptials of the eternal King. There we shall be the food of God, for He will be well pleased with us; and He will be our food; for, when we behold His glory face to face, we shall delight in Him. And in this way will be fulfilled the saying of the prophet, 'I shall be satisfied, when Thy glory shall appear'.[3]

CHAPTER 15

Of the food of divine contemplation, and how after death we shall be the food of God, and He will be ours

Let us then conclude with the highest degree of perfection and say: (the tree of wisdom) *feeds by contemplation.*

Through contemplation it gives food. (God Himself) is food. This is the refection of which the psalmist says, 'Thou shalt fill me with joy in Thy face; in Thy right hand are delights, even to the end'.[4]

[1] Vulg. Cant. V, 1; cf. A.V. Song of Sol. iv, 16.
[2] See Song of Sol. v, 1.
[3] Vulg. Ps. xvi, 15; cf. A.V. xvii, 15.
[4] Vulg. Ps. xv, 11; cf. A.V. xvi, 11.

CHAPTER 16

Of the mystery of the numbers seven and eight that make fifteen

There, now, the tree of our wisdom reaches its full growth by fifteen stages. This number is, however, part of a great mystery, in the first place because it is made up of seven and eight. Seven denotes this present life which runs through seven days; eight, which comes after seven, signifies eternal life. Seven, therefore, refers to the Old Testament, in which temporal benefits are promised; whereas eight is appropriate to the New Testament, in which we are bidden to hope for everlasting ones. Let wisdom grow, then, through seven and eight. Let it begin with seven, and attain its perfecting through eight. Let the first wisdom be to ask God for earthly benefits; let the second and chief be to desire God from God.

Again, twice fifteen makes thirty, and wisdom, if it be joined to love for God and for one's neighbour, is doubled till it leads us to conformity to 'the age of the fullness of Christ'.[1]

Again, the middle number in fifteen is eight, and it has seven either side of it. And it is clear enough that seven has reference to rest, for this reason primarily that 'on the seventh day the Lord rested from all the work that He had made'.[2] Again, God renews through the prophet his promise to those who love Him, 'sabbath for sabbath and month for month'[3]—that is to say, rest for rest and perfection for perfection; for rest of soul, rest of both soul and body; for the rest in which they now submit to evils, a rest in which they know no ills; and again, for the perfection of work, the perfection of reward. For when He says 'sabbath for sabbath' it is the same as if He said 'rest for rest', and when He says 'month for month' it is the same as if He said 'perfection for perfection'.

Our first rest, therefore, our first sabbath, must be to cease

[1] Cf. Vulg. Eph. iv, 13; cf. A.V. loc. cit.
[2] See Vulg. Gen. ii, 2 and cf. A.V. loc. cit.
[3] See Vulg. Isa. lxvi, 23; cf. A.V. loc. cit.

from evil in this present life, so that we may merit to obtain our second sabbath, and to rest with Christ to all eternity.

But he who in this way decides to keep sabbath from evil must suffer many troubles in this world ere he can reach that sabbath that is yet to be. So in the tree of wisdom, at the eighth stage, which comes between seven and seven as between rest and rest, the endurance of hardship is placed right at the very centre of the whole, when it is said that 'it is strengthened by charity'. For a sturdy charity is needed in face of great tribulations. And this is what the Lord counselled in the gospel about endurance of suffering, when after enumerating seven beatitudes He said in the eighth: 'Blessed are those who suffer persecution for righteousness' sake: for theirs is the kingdom of heaven.'[1] For what is said there, 'Blessed are those who suffer persecution for righteousness' sake', means the same as what is said here, that it (i.e. the tree of wisdom) is strengthened by charity.

But now, in following up the explanation of subordinate matters, we have strayed somewhat far from the subject that we took in hand. Wherefore we crave your indulgence on this account; for, truth to tell, in writing this treatise we have come on many things that simply had to be put down. And yet I do not blush to confess my folly in so doing.

Now, therefore, let us return to our subject, and pursue the matter of the building of the ark of wisdom.

[1] Vulg. Matt. v, 10; cf. A.V. loc. cit.

Book IV

CHAPTER I[1]

Of the house of God, where it must be built, of what material, and who is the Builder

We wish to speak about the building of the house of God, if perchance we, unworthy as we are to speak about so great a matter, prove capable of doing so as it deserves. Yet even if we are thus insufficient of ourselves, He, of whom we are not fit, I do not say to speak but even to think except He aid us, is able to make me sufficient.

First we must specify the place wherein the Lord's house must be built; then we must tell you of its material. The place is the heart of man, and the material is pure thoughts. Let no one make excuse, let no one say: '*I* cannot build a house for the Lord, my slender means are not sufficient to meet such great demands. Exile and pilgrim as I am, and dwelling in a country not my own, I lack even a site. This is a work for kings. This is a work for many people. How should *I* build a house for the Lord?' O man, why do you think like that? That is not what your God requires from you. He is not telling you to buy a piece of land from someone else, in order to extend His courts. He wants to dwell in your own heart—extend and enlarge that! Enlarge it, I say, for the Lord is great and cannot dwell in a strait space. Enlarge your heart, therefore, so that you may be able to contain Him whom the whole world cannot contain. Enlarge your heart, so that you may be worthy to have God as your guest, and not to have Him as a guest for only a single night (as is the custom with men) but as one who dwells there for ever. Enlarge your heart therefore. Where you yourself fail in doing this, He will enlarge it for you. A man whose heart had

[1] Chapter 1 = MPL, clxxvi, cols. 663–5 (Bk. IV, ch. 1).

been thus enlarged by Him said to Him once, 'I have run the way of Thy commandments, since Thou hast enlarged my heart'.[1]

And what shall I say of the cost? There is no need to cross the seas and search out unknown places to procure precious stones and choice marbles. There is no need to ship tall cedars out of Lebanon across deep seas, or gather together I know not how many thousands of craftsmen, such as would drain the resources even of kings. None of these things is required of you. You will build a house for the Lord your God *in and of yourself*. He will be the craftsman, your heart the site, your thoughts the materials. Do not take fright because of your own lack of skill; He who requires this of you is a skilful builder, and He chooses others to be builders too. We have learnt of many who were trained by Him from the testimony of Holy Scripture. He taught Noah to build the ark.[2] He showed Moses the pattern on which he was to build the ark (of the covenant).[3] He taught Bezaleel.[4] He enlightened Solomon with wisdom, that he might build a temple to His name.[5] Paul the apostle too He made a builder,[6] and many others whom it would take a long time to enumerate. And in any case no one was wise who had not learnt from Him, and no one remained unskilled who was fortunate enough to be His pupil.

But if you would like to hear something of what He did: He created everything you see from nothing. He it was who fashioned the marvellous framework of the world. He contrived the shapes and forms that were to be assumed by every single thing, and gave all things their beauty. You may well judge, then, what He can do in things invisible, who has disposed things visible in such a marvellous way.

Call upon Him, therefore, beg and beseech Him, that He may deign to teach you too. Call upon Him, love Him; for to call

[1] Vulg. Ps. cxviii, 32; cf. A.V. Ps. cxix, 32.
[2] See Gen. vi, 14–16.
[3] See Exod. xxv, 10–16.
[4] See Exod. xxxvi, 1 ff.
[5] See 1 Kings iv, 29–vi, 38.
[6] See e.g. 1 Cor. iii, 10 and 2 Cor. vi, 1.

upon Him is to love Him. Love Him, therefore, and He Himself will come to you and teach you, as He has promised those who love Him. 'If a man love Me, he will keep My words: and My Father will love him, and We will come to him, and make Our abode with him.'[1] I take this to mean that the Lover of pure hearts cannot abide in us, unless He has first made Himself a dwelling in us. For in truth He is Himself the wisdom whereof it is said, 'Wisdom hath builded her house',[2] and in another place the selfsame wisdom shows where and out of what material the house has been made, saying, 'I, wisdom, dwell in counsel and am present in reasonable thoughts'.[3] And in another place the soul of the righteous is described as wisdom's seat.[4]

It is clear, therefore, that wisdom builds herself a house in the heart of man out of reasonable thoughts.

CHAPTER 2[5]

How that there are two builders in the building of the house of God[6]

Those, then, are the three things, the place and the material and the Builder. And, as I have said, the place is the heart of man and the material is the thoughts thereof. There are, however, two employed upon the work, God, and the man himself; and these two work together. For God, who condescends to dwell in man, does not disdain to make Himself a dwelling with him. So a man ought not to give way to hopelessness at the thought of his own inexperience or weakness; rather, he should look to Him who is good enough to work along with him. For God is strength and wisdom; and it cannot be that anyone who has strength from Him should faint, or that he should lack for knowledge when wisdom is there, especially since He who

[1] John, xiv, 23.
[2] Prov. ix, 1.
[3] Vulg. Prov. viii, 12; cf. A.V. loc. cit.
[4] A reference perhaps to Wisd. of Sol. vii, 27.
[5] Chapter 2 = MPL, clxxvi, col. 665 (Bk. IV, ch. 1).
[6] See Vulg. Ps. cxxvi, 1; A.V. Ps. cxxvii, 1.

works along with us when we do good, and He who grants us the desire and the power to do good when we are not doing it, are One and the Same. Indeed the work of God in us is with us, and our work in ourselves is from Him, as His gift.

This being said, let us come to the subject that we had intended, namely that you, who now know where and with what material and with whom you have to work, may next learn how to do it.

CHAPTER 3[1]

That in every building three things must be considered

In every building there are three things that call for primary consideration, the order, the arrangement, and the precise measurement—that is to say, exactly where it starts and where it finishes. And so it remains for us to find out what sort of order and arrangement there should be in our thoughts, so that a house for God may be built out of them.

After that, we must carefully consider how this house, which we are building for God to live in, can be given a precise measurement when He Himself, the Resident, is God, the infinite and measureless. But let us begin with the matter that we first decided to examine.

CHAPTER 4[2]

Of the order of building, and how we may acquire steady and peaceful thoughts

As far as we can see, the number of all things is infinite, for it is beyond our comprehension. But where there is no limit, there can be no certitude; and where there is no certitude, confusion reigns. And, where confusion reigns, there is no order.

It is for this reason that, when we let our hearts run after

[1] Chapter 3 = MPL, clxxvi, col. 665 (Bk. IV, ch. 1).
[2] Chapter 4 = MPL, clxxvi, cols. 665–6 (Bk. IV, ch. 2).

earthly things without restraint, a multitude of vain thoughts arises, so that our mind becomes so divided that even the order of our native discrimination is disturbed. For, since the worldly things that we desire so unrestrainedly are infinite, the thoughts that we conceive when we remember them cannot be finite. As from moment to moment they arise one after another in so many different ways, even we ourselves cannot give any account of whence or how they enter or leave the mind.

If, then, we want to have ordered, steady, peaceful thoughts, let us make it our business to restrain our hearts from this immoderate distraction.

This can be done, provided we give ourselves certain definite objects to engage our attention seriously and to occupy our thoughts. There are three possibilities: we can divide our attention between a number of things, we can concentrate on one thing only, or we can change within limits. Of these possibilities, there is one that we cannot achieve, and one to which we ought not to submit. So that leaves only one, namely that, since we cannot at present be really constant in heart, we should for the time being at least recollect our hearts from their unrestrained distractions. And in this way, while we are always striving to be less unstable, we may be getting ever nearer to some semblance of true stability.

And to make what we are saying clearer by means of an illustration, let us imagine three things, one at the bottom, another at the top, and the third in the middle. At the bottom let us put the world, at the top God, and in the middle let us place the human soul. Then let us contemplate the vast and horrible confusion that prevails in that world down there, and the infinite distraction of the minds of men. But up above, with God, there is perpetual, unshakable stability. Having seen these, let us picture to ourselves a human soul rising out of this world towards God and, as it rises, gathering itself ever more and more into a unity. Then we shall be able to see in a spiritual manner the form of our ark, which was broad at the bottom, and narrowed gradually as it rose, till at the peak it came to measure a single cubit only. In the same way, as we rise from out of this deep, this vale of tears, we grow steadily in the virtues as by certain ordered stages in our hearts, and we are gradually drawn towards a unity, until we attain even to that simple oneness, that true simplicity and everlasting changelessness, that is in God. No one becomes perfect suddenly, but everyone who is making progress is on the way towards perfection, since as long as he is capable of further progress he has not yet achieved the fullness of perfection.

At this point, we may choose to consider the manner of our reintegration.

CHAPTER 5[1]

Why man returns to God through many toils

Nothing is impossible to Almighty God, and if He so willed, He could without delay translate those upon whom He intended to have mercy straight from the toils, the difficulties, and the dangers of this present life that is so crowded with temptations, to the changelessness of the eternal life. What He does will, however, is that His chosen should go through the purgation of divers troubles and numerous trials. Thus as they return to Him by way of many sorrows, they may understand how far they had strayed from Him by sinning. For when, not as men translated but as men led back, they traverse by repentance the road along which they had gone away by sinning, they realize as it were from the daily fatigue of the journey, that they have been brought back as from afar. And all this is done that they may appreciate the grace of God, that they may love Him the more ardently as they perceive that, even as He promised through Isaiah the prophet, saying, 'I will bring thy seed from the east, and gather thee from the west. I will say to the north, "Give up"; and to the south, "Keep not back: bring My sons from afar and My daughters from the ends of the earth" ',[2] so He never forsook them, even when they were far off.

[1] Chapter 5 = MPL, clxxvi, cols. 666–7 (Bk. IV, ch. 2).
[2] Isa. xliii, 5 ff.

Every one of you, who remembers where he was and recognizes where he is, may be led perhaps to see from his own case how through God's mercy man is brought from afar, and reintegrated after being scattered abroad.

CHAPTER 6[1]

How the soul may form the habit of stability

It remains for us to consider what those things are, of which we spoke just now, which it behoves a soul to practise, so that it may gradually form the habit of withdrawing itself from the distraction of this world, to the intent that it may rise up strengthened to that supreme stability,[2] the contemplation of God.

The matter may be viewed like this. All the works of God were made for man, both those that belong to man's original creation, and those that were done for his restoration.[3] The creation of the world, of heaven and earth and all the things that are said to have been made by God from the beginning, was with a view to the creation of man. To his restoration belongs the Incarnation of the Word, and all those things which, since the beginning, preceded the Incarnation either to foreshadow or foretell it, together with those that came after it until the end of the world, with a view to preaching or believing in it.

But whereas in the case of the first works, which are related to man's creation, God is the God of all, since He Himself created them and bestowed these temporal blessings indifferently on good and bad alike, in the case of those which belong to man's restoration He did not will to be the God of all men, but only of those whom, before time was, He of His good will meant to choose, that He might call them in due time, and

[1] Chapter 6 = MPL, clxxvi, col. 667 (Bk. IV, ch. 2–3).

[2] Hugh means by *stabilitas* the changelessness of God, rather than stability in its common English sense.

[3] Cf. *De Sacramentis*, lib. I, par. vi and viii (MPL, clxxvi, cols. 263–83 and 306–18); and *De Vanitate Mundi*, lib. II (MPL, clxxvi, col. 716B).

justify and glorify them in His beloved Son, our Lord Jesus Christ. That is why in Holy Scripture God calls Himself the God of particular individuals, as in this passage, 'I am the God of Abraham, the God of Isaac and the God of Jacob'.[1] For, as we have said, He who created all has not redeemed them all, but saves some in His mercy and condemns others in His justice. So those of His works that were done for the restoration of man do not belong to all men, but to those only who are being saved. And as they do not belong to all men, so also they were not done in all places, nor have they come to all men's knowledge; but they were done at certain particular places and times, and involved particular individuals chosen in the hidden depths of the divine counsel. For although in His omnipotence God could have employed many methods to restore mankind, this, the most fitted to our weakness, was the one that He preferred; so that the work of His mercy might be fulfilled not only mightily and righteously, but wisely too.

CHAPTER 7[2]

How man returns to God through faith, the grace of God arousing his free will

The first man forsook his Maker, although through contemplation he beheld Him present. Man now seeks through faith the Maker whose face he does not see. The first man had the power to stand firm without any difficulty, and fell by his own choice. But now, when a man rises of his own free choice, he returns to God only through trials. The divine economy of our restoration is, therefore, supremely well ordered, in that he who fell of his own choice should rise, not as compelled to do so, but of his own choice too, and that he, who through free will was rendered sick, should not recover his health until such time as by his own free will he should desire healing.

Yet it is not of ourselves to will, but it is rather God who

[1] Exod. iii, 6.

[2] Chapter 7 = MPL, clxxvi, cols. 667–8 (Bk. IV, ch. 3).

works this in us. For the grace of God goes before and stirs our will to desire its healing, when of itself it could only make us more infirm. This, then, is what is happening to God's chosen ones in this present life as a preparation for their future happiness; that a man, finding himself in this unhappy condition, should be found worthy to rise up to happiness, just as formerly, when he enjoyed that happiness, he deserved to sink down to this misery.

Yet only that desert whereby man merited to be unhappy was of man himself. *This* merit, by the which he merits everlasting bliss, is not of man, but God's grace works it in him.

CHAPTER 8[1]

Why God so manifests Himself to man, that nonetheless He remains hidden from him

Not without reason is it, therefore, that when God calls man back after sin from the blindness of ignorance, He so qualifies his apprehension of Himself as to let Himself be known of him, and yet at the same time always to be hid from him. For if He showed Himself so openly to men that none could be in any doubt about Him, faith would have no merit and unbelief no place. So He makes Himself known that faith may be fostered; and He continues hidden lest unbelief be overcome. He remains hidden, that faith may be proved; He makes Himself known, that unbelief may be convinced. For in that believers have the opportunity of doubt, and unbelievers likewise the opportunity of faith, if they would only take it, the former get the reward of faith, and the latter with equal justice the punishment of unbelief.

For it pleased God to make man first deserve the blessedness which He was going to give him as a free gift, yet in such wise that both the merit and its recompense derived from Him. So He puts off giving that which He is going to give—full health, full knowledge, full felicity, and in the meantime enlightens our

[1] Chapter 8 = MPL, clxxvi, cols. 668–9 (Bk. IV, ch. 3–4).

blindness through faith, so that, advancing by its means, we may deserve to come into His open glory.

This, then, is how from the beginning God has spoken with the few, occasionally, darkly, and in secret. If we study the Scriptures, we shall find that God hardly ever speaks to a crowd of people. Rather, so often as He willed to make Himself known to men, He showed Himself, not to nations and peoples, but to individuals, or at most to a few, and to them when they were separated from the common ways of men by the silence of the night, maybe, or in the fields, or in deserts and mountains. In this way He spoke with Noah, with Abraham, with Isaac, with Jacob, with Moses, with Samuel, with David, and with all the prophets.

When at length He appeared in flesh, though He spoke openly to the world, nevertheless He led His disciples apart on the mountain to show them His glory.[1] To the disciples also in another place He said, 'to you it is given to know the mystery of the kingdom of God, but to the rest in parables'.[2] And again: 'What I tell you in darkness, that tell ye in the light; and what ye hear in the ear, that preach ye from the roof-tops.'[3] Neither did He give the Law to the ancient people in Egypt, until He had led them out into the wilderness apart. And even there He did not do so openly to all; it was Moses alone who went up into the mountain to receive the Law.[4]

Why is it, then, that God always speaks in secret, if not because He calls us into what is hidden? And why does He speak with a few, if not that He may gather us together? Weigh these two things that I have said, *He gathers us together*, and *He calls us into what is hidden*.

[1] Mark ix, 2, 8 and parallels.
[2] See Matt. xiii, 11.
[3] Vulg. Matt. x, 27; cf. A.V. loc. cit.
[4] Exod. xix, 17 ff.

CHAPTER 9[1]

Why God speaks outwardly to man, why secretly, and why obscurely

Before he sinned, the first man had no need for God to speak to him outwardly, for he possessed an ear within his heart by which he could hear God's voice after a spiritual manner. But when he opened his outward ear to listen to the serpent's guile,[2] he closed his inward ear to the voice of God.

Since, therefore, man has lost the power to hear God speak within him, He, when He recalls us to Himself, cries outwardly. But when He speaks, He always withdraws Himself, as if He wished to hide; (and this He does) so that He may reprove man's heart by the fact that He speaks of Himself, and draw it to Himself by the fact that He escapes to hide. For He arouses our desire that He may increase it, quickening the love of Him in us by speaking, and goading us to follow Him by running away. For such is the heart of man, that if it cannot gain possession of the thing it loves, it burns the more with longing.

This is how in the Song of Songs the Bridegroom comes and stands behind the wall, and looks through the window and the lattices,[3] as it were hiding and not hiding. He puts His hand through the opening[4] and touches the bride, He calls her in a low voice, in a whisper, saying: 'Come, My friend, My dove! Lo, the winter is past, the rain is over and gone; the flowers have appeared, the voice of the turtle is heard in our land.'[5] And she, hearing the Bridegroom there, rises forthwith, she makes haste and unbolts the door; and, as though she were just going to receive Him, she stretches out her arms in readiness. She can hardly bear it, scarce endure it, barely wait. Her soul melts within, her spirit burns, her inmost being is on fire, she is jubilant, she rejoices, she dances and is gay, she fairly runs to

[1] Chapter 9 = MPL, clxxvi, cols. 669–70 (Bk. IV, ch. 4).
[2] Gen. iii, 1–7.
[3] Song of Sol. ii, 9.
[4] Ibid. v, 4.
[5] See Vulg. Cant. ii, 10–12; cf. A.V. Song of Sol. loc. cit.

meet Him who comes to her. But He, just when she thought she held Him, evades her, and suddenly, as though He slipped from her embrace, takes flight.

What can this mean? When no one seeks Him, He sets out in search; when He is not called, He comes. But when He is sought, He slips away; when He is called, He flees. If He does not love her, why then does He come? Or, if He loves her, why then does He flee? He does indeed love her, and therefore He comes. But it is not here that He loves her, and therefore He flees. What do I mean by saying that it is 'not here' that He loves her? I mean that it is not in this world, in this age, on this earth or in this country, in this exile. But He calls us to *His* country, to His own land; for such a love as this is ill suited to this land of ours, the squalor of the place would be an insult to love. A fair love demands a pleasant place.

So, when He says, 'The flowers have appeared in our land, the flowering vines have yielded their fragrance, the voice of the turtle is heard in our land',[1] He is speaking of His own country and praising His own land; so that we may burn to see such a place, and long for such a country, and follow after Him.

There it is that He loves us, there He desires to enjoy our love, there He asks us to embrace Him, there He does not flee from those who follow Him, but waits for them to come. He offers Himself, therefore, though He is not sought, that He may kindle us with love towards Himself. When He is sought, He flees, so as to lead us to run after Him. For if He had not first shown Himself to us, no one would love Him. And if He did not flee when He was sought, nobody would pursue Him. 'The flowers', He says, 'have appeared in our land'—'in *our* land', not 'in Mine', for He would share it with us. It is as though He said: 'I am a faithful messenger to you. I have seen that of which I testify, I have heard what I tell. Do not fear, do not doubt, do not linger. Follow Me whither I call, for your place is there, whence I come. Here you have no abiding city. It is a foreign land that you are living in. You have come here from somewhere else. If you remembered your homeland, you would

[1] Cf. Vulg. Cant. ii, 12; A.V. Song of Sol. loc. cit.

certainly not love the place of your exile! Therefore I Myself have come to lead you hence, not to stay here with you. And this is why I cry to you from hiding, for I want only to be known, not to stay. I call you from afar, for I am in a hurry to return. To make Myself heard, it was enough for Me to come forth; I should have judged it a personal loss had I gone the rest of the way, for all delay is hard to bear. The flowers have appeared in our land. Seeing Me thus hastening away, know how much you too ought to hasten. I should not have come, if I had not loved you. I should not have fled, but that I wished to draw you after Me.'

This is the reason why God always speaks in secret. The reason why He speaks darkly is akin to it. As in the law and the prophets, so in the gospel also He spoke by parables and riddles. For it is fitting that the secrets of the mystical sense should be hidden beneath figures of speech; for were they always open to all, they would be quickly cheapened. In this way truth keeps the faithful busy in searching it out, and at the same time continues hidden, lest it be found by unbelievers. When it is hard to find, it fires the former with yet greater longing; but it blinds the latter when it cannot be found at all. From the same cause, therefore, believers make progress and unbelievers fall away; since the former come to know the truth through humble listening and faithful searching out of the word of God, while the latter, by neglecting, despising, or wrongly understanding it never reach the truth.

We have now said why God speaks darkly and in secret. It remains to tell you why He speaks with few and seldom.

CHAPTER 10[1]

How the first man's nature was constituted, how he became blind and unstable, and why God speaks with few, and only on occasion

The first man's nature was so ordained and constituted by God that the soul, which governed the body, should fulfil its

[1] Chapter 10 = MPL, cols. 670–2 (Bk. IV, ch. 5).

outward service to the body, certainly, but that, by means of reason, it should always be directed inwardly towards its Maker. It should—in other words—move the bodily members to external activity by giving them sense-life, but direct its attention and desire within to its Maker alone, and do nothing outwardly that did not originate in love for Him, or bear some relation to that love. Charity was thus to command, reason to direct, and the sensitive faculties to fulfil and complete his every act.

As long, therefore, as man retained this order in his nature, he still remained within himself unmoved in purpose and in love, although his external activity subjected him to change. For he had one only purpose and did all things to one end. He loved one only thing, and the motive of all his desires and actions had reference to it. The depth of his spirit[1] was always unfailingly turned towards that one object, his Maker.

Never, therefore, could he be in any doubt about his Maker, who was ever present within him by contemplation. The sight of Him enlightened his mind with knowledge, and made him to rise up and to lie down with love. But after he was cast out from before God's face because of his transgression, he became blind and unstable, blind through mental ignorance and unstable through fleshly concupiscence. Both of these he passed on to his entire posterity, and to them every evil owes its origin. For through ignorance men at last sank so low that they did not acknowledge their Creator, and either thought that God did not exist at all, or else believed in the divinity of things that were not gods. And through concupiscence they were bewildered and led astray by countless falsehoods. For since men were thus subject to the darkness of ignorance and unaware of the existence of any other invisible good things, it was

[1] *Acies mentis*, as it were the pupil of the soul's eye, an Augustinian notion whose origin as a metaphor from sight is most clearly suggested in *Enarratio in Psalmum cxliv* (MPL, xxxvii, col. 1872). Thus we get: *Nondum habet ad aeterna contemplanda idoneam mentis aciem qui visibilibus tantum, id est temporalibus credit.*, *De Vera Religione*, ch. liv (MPL, xxxiv, col. 169). It is essentially the same as that *fond* of the soul which later spiritual writers will call the *pointe suprême*. St. François de Sales, *Traité de l'amour de Dieu*, I, xii.

inevitable that they should lose control of themselves through the lust for earthly things which can be seen.

God, therefore, wishing to collect our hearts from this distracted state, and to recall them to the contemplation of interior joys, speaks outwardly, in order that He may exhort us to return into ourselves. But because a mind accustomed to things that can be seen cannot so soon rise up to unseen things, He Himself decided to perform some miracles that could be seen, whereby our attraction for Him might be strengthened and His love towards us proved. Now these things have a special connexion with man's restoration. For the things that were done with a view to the making of man show us chiefly their Creator's power; while those whose purpose was man's redemption are mainly connected with His love.

God, therefore, did these things to show what manner of love He bore us, and to call us back from the love of this world to that of Himself. Hence, too, He chose to limit the number of these works, lest, if there were no end to them, our soul that was to be unified should become preoccupied with them. Yet He decided to make them many, that the same soul, that could not yet endure a total lack of change, might find delight in their variety.

This is the reason why He chose one people and one place, in which to begin the mysteries which concerned the salvation not of one people only, but of the whole world. He wanted to commend unity everywhere, and to recall the soul of man, inside and out, back to unity; for His intention was that even as the salvation of all men comes by the single Saviour, so also the beginning of salvation should come from a single people and a single place. For He who made all things for our sake undoubtedly acted as He knew was best for us.

God, however, did these things partly through men, partly through angels, and partly of Himself. He did most of them through men, many through angels, a few of Himself; so that, just as the human soul makes progress by climbing in its thought from the deeds of men to the deeds of angels, and from the deeds of angels to the acts of God, so also it may gradually grow accustomed to unifying itself, and to approaching nearer to the true simplicity, in proportion as it gets further off from multiplicity.

So, then, when God by speaking with the few (and that but seldom) draws our hearts to unity, and by speaking darkly and in secret draws them upwards to Himself, what else is He doing —if I may so say—but producing in our hearts the form of an invisible ark?

CHAPTER 11[1]

That the elect are affected by the works of creation and restoration in one way, and the reprobate in another

Therefore, although He made all things for the sake of man, His will was that the things He made for the service of those who were in health should be different from those that were intended to afford a medicine for the sick. For the world could keep a man in health, but it could not make a sick man better. Therefore, after that first creation of the things that were to minister to those who stood, it was necessary to make others which should raise the fallen. These are nobler than the first, as being the more necessary; and, as they are nobler, they take longer. For the former were made in six days, the latter in six ages, six days for the creation of things, six ages for the restoration of man.

You must understand, however, that the elect assess the works of God in one way, the reprobate in another. For the elect reckon the works of restoration as superior to those of the first creation, because those were made for bondage, but the former were for our salvation. The reprobate, by contrast, love the works of creation more than those of restoration, because they seek present satisfaction, and not future bliss. The pagan philosophers, in searching out the nature of things with curiosity—that is, in inquiring into the works of creation, have become futile in their thoughts; but Christian sages, by medi-

[1] Chapter 11 = MPL, clxxvi, col. 672 (Bk. IV, ch. 5–6).

tating constantly upon the works of restoration, drive every vanity from theirs. The elect, considering their restoration, are kindled with the fire of love divine; the reprobate, with their false love of the loveliness of things created, grow cold in the love of God. The reprobate, immersing their thoughts in transitory things, forget their Creator. But the elect cannot forget Him, whose mercy in their restoration they have constantly in mind. The reprobate, while panting after temporary things, lose their perception of the things eternal; but the elect, while pondering God's temporal benefits, advance to knowledge of the everlasting ones. By visible things the reprobate fall from those that are invisible; but by the visible the elect climb up to the invisible.

CHAPTER 12[1]

What is the unseen world, what is the flood therein, and what is the ark in this flood

You must understand, however, that the visible things from which the elect mount up are different from those by means of which they do so. They mount up *from* the works of creation, *by means of* those of restoration, *to* the Author of creation and of restoration. But those ascents must be conceived not outwardly but inwardly, as taking place by means of steps within the heart, which go from strength to strength. This we may perhaps be better able to understand if it is put as follows.

Just as we have drawn a distinction between the two kinds of works, the works of creation and the works of restoration, so let us understand that there are two worlds, the seen and the unseen, the former being this whole scheme of things which we see with our bodily eyes, and the latter the heart of man, which we cannot see. And as in the days of Noah when the waters of the flood covered the whole earth, the ark alone was borne upon the waters, and was not only unsinkable but actually rose higher as the waters rose, so now let us see that the desire of this world

[1] Chapter 12 = op. cit., cols. 672–3 (Bk. IV, ch. 6–7).

in the heart of man is as it were the waters of the flood, while the ark which is borne upon them is the faith of Christ, which treads down transitory pleasures and aspires to those everlasting benefits that are above.

The lust of this world is likened, therefore, to the waters because it is liquid and slippery, because like water that runs downhill it always seeks the lowest level, and because it makes those who pursue it unstable and disintegrated. If a man enters his own heart, he will see how this concupiscence always flows downwards to the things that pass, while faith is directed towards the lasting benefits that are above.

CHAPTER 13[1]

In what sense faith and concupiscence are said to dwell in the heart of man

How come we, however, to assert that both concupiscence and faith dwell in the heart, though Scripture says that concupiscence dwells in the flesh, and only faith in the heart? We do so for no other reason than that we are said to lust with the flesh when we lust with the heart after a fleshly manner. To lust and to believe are alike the properties of the heart, but the character it has from loving earthly things differs from that which it derives from seeking after heavenly ones. And so concupiscence is from below, faith from above. Concupiscence arises in the heart from the flesh; faith is not of the flesh at all, but is breathed into the heart by God. Wherefore when the Lord is praising Peter's confession of faith, He says, 'Flesh and blood hath not revealed this to thee, but My Father who is in heaven'.[2] But of concupiscence Paul says, 'it is not I that do it, but sin that dwelleth in me'. And what 'in me' means he specifies in the same place when he says, 'I know that in me'—that is, in my flesh—'dwelleth no good thing'.[3] Again, he tells us in

[1] Chapter 13 = MPL, clxxvi, cols. 673–4 (Bk. IV, ch. 7).
[2] See Matt. xvi, 17.
[3] Rom. vii, 17 ff.

another place what that sin actually is, which he has said dwells in the flesh. 'Walk in the Spirit, and ye shall not fulfil the desires of the flesh'[1]—calling concupiscence 'the desires of the flesh'.

Concupiscence, then, dwells in the flesh, that is, low down in the heart, but faith dwells not in the flesh but in the spirit—that is, up above in the heart. We should, however, be careful to observe that, when the apostle says, 'Walk in the spirit and ye shall not *fulfil* the lust of the flesh'—and did not say, 'ye shall not *feel* them', he plainly teaches that concupiscence resulting from his corrupt origin is inevitably present in every man, as long as he is in this life, but that it is not impossible for anyone, with the help of God's grace, to refrain from consenting to it. Wherefore he says elsewhere, 'Let not sin reign in your mortal body',[2] as if to say: 'It cannot be that there should be no sin—that is, no stirring of sin, no goad of vice or prick of concupiscence in your mortal body; but, God helping you, it *is* possible that it should not reign there, should not be in command. It is impossible that you should not feel it, but there is no necessity for you to yield to it.'

Everyone, then, is subject to a kind of flood of concupiscence in his own heart, from which nobody can be released save by the ark of faith, (and)[3] where a bad man walking on dry land is drowned and a good man, submerged in the depths of the sea, escapes unhurt. It is indeed a dangerous tempest that goes on inside us, and woe to him who is imperilled by it! For him, who within himself is tossed by the billows of concupiscence and engulfed by the ever-hungry whirlpool of his lusts, there is no safe harbour, no secure anchorage, no tranquil calm.

[1] See Gal. v, 16.

[2] Rom. vi, 12.

[3] In both Migne and the manuscript this clause 'where . . . unhurt' stands between full stops. It can therefore be taken either with what precedes it or with what follows it; but the former seems to make the better sense.

CHAPTER 14[1]

Of the three kinds of people who in divers manners abide in the flood of concupiscence

Here we may well consider three kinds of people, those who have a flood within them, but no ark; those who have both a flood and an ark, but are not in the ark; and those who in the flood both have an ark and stay in it.

In the flood without an ark are the unbelievers, who are entangled in their lusts and do not know that there is any life except this transitory one.

In the flood, having an ark but not abiding in it, are those who through faith have learnt already to believe that an unchanging life will supervene upon the finish of this changing one, but, putting the thought of that behind them, give their souls over to the delight of temporal things. For the Scripture says, 'where your treasure is, there will your heart be also'.[2] Where your desire is, there also is your heart. Where your delight is, there also is your thought; and where your thought is, there is the dwelling of the inner man. For according to the inner man, everyone is said to dwell in that place where he dwells in thought. They, therefore, who find their delight in the vanity of this world, are shipwrecked men within, though they may have the ark of faith.

But to say nothing of other lovers of the world, how many educated people do we see nowadays, who would like to be called Christians, come to church with the rest of the faithful, and receive the sacraments of Christ, while in their heart they are more often thinking of Saturn and of Jupiter, of Hercules or Mars, or of Achilles and Hector, Pollux and Castor, Socrates, Plato, and Aristotle, than of Christ and His saints. They love the poets' trifles, and either neglect the truth of Holy Scripture or—what is worse—laugh at it or despise it. Let such as these

[1] Chapter 14 = MPL, clxxvi, col. 674 (Bk. IV, ch. 8).
[2] Matt. vi, 21.

see what good it will do them to come to church outwardly, while in their hearts they are committing fornication against the faith. I tell them openly, that at the last those to whom by their hearts' affection they unite themselves will be their fellows, and they will share the punishment of those whose life they here hold dear. What good does it do them to have faith, and not abide therein? What does it profit them to have a sound ship, and I will not say merely to suffer shipwreck in the waves, but actually to bring the wreck about? What is the use of knowing the truth and loving what is false?

The true believers are not of that sort. Would you like to know what kind of men they are? Listen to the description of one of them, then, and understand that they are all the same; for those who are one in the truth cannot be unlike. Hear, then, what is said of him. 'The law of his God is in his heart'[1]—that is, he has an ark inside. And, in case this should not be enough, listen also to this. 'His will is in the law of the Lord'[2]—that is, he lives in the ark. He is the perfect man, who loves what he believes, so that his faith is that which works by love, which overcomes the world.[3]

CHAPTER 15[4]

What are the great and wide sea, the creeping things thereof, and the ships that cross it

This is the ark in which we must be saved, which can be borne upon the waters, but by no means sunk by them, because it uses this world for its needs, but does not succumb to it through cupidity. This is what the psalm says, 'this great sea in whose widespread arms are reptiles without number, animals small and great. Ships shall sail across it'.[5] For the 'sea' in us is the concupiscence of this world, wherein, if pleasures can be

[1] Ps. xxxvii, 31.
[2] See Vulg. Ps. i, 2; cf. A.V. loc. cit.
[3] See Gal. v, 6 and 1 John v, 4.
[4] Chapter 15 = MPL, clxxvi, cols. 674–5 (Bk. IV, ch. 8).
[5] Vulg. Ps. ciii, 25–6; cf. A.V. Ps. civ, 25–6.

found, they are mixed up with many bitter things that flow downwards in our heart according to our bodily temperament. The 'reptiles' are fleshly thoughts misshapen by the foulness of sundry forms of vice. When we admit these to our hearts without restraint, we fill our inmost being as it were with monstrous reptiles. The 'ship' is that spiritual ark which is our faith, which being raised up within us rides upon the lusts of this world. The verse says 'ships' on account of the number of souls. For many souls are one soul on account of their unity in faith and love; and one faith is many faiths on account of the number of the faithful, in the way that we say 'thy faith hath made thee whole',[1] and 'my faith' and 'his faith', although there is only one catholic faith.

CHAPTER 16[2]

How that every man is in the flood of concupiscence, but the good and the bad are so in different ways

One only ship of faith, therefore, crosses the sea, one only ark escapes the flood; and, if we would be saved, not only must it be in us, but we must be in it. And let no one say, trusting to his good conscience, 'What do I want with this ark? The flood of concupiscence has dried up in me.' Yes, he who lives outside does not know what is going on inside; but let a man return to his own heart, and he will find there a stormy ocean lashed by the fierce billows of overwhelming passions and desires, which swamp the soul as often as by consent they bring it into subjection. For there is this flood in every man, as long as he lives in this corruptible life, where the flesh lusts against the spirit. Or rather, every man is in this flood, but the good are in it as those borne in ships upon the sea, whereas the bad are in it as shipwrecked persons at the mercy of the waves.

In the good, the waters of this flood do indeed begin to lessen in this life, and they abate in individuals more or less

[1] Mark v, 34.

[2] Chapter 16 = MPL, clxxvi, col. 675 (Bk. IV, ch. 8).

according to the difference of their graces. But the earth of the heart of man can never be entirely dried out while this life lasts. And therefore, when the dove is sent out, she does not find here a place to rest her foot, but returns to the ark again and again.[1] For while the pure soul can find no safe foothold for its affection in this world, it is afraid to be away for long from the safeguard of inward meditation.

If, however, on occasion it has gone out in thought, like the dove that flies away and goes far off, it returns swiftly to the solitude of its own conscience,[2] and there it rests from the turmoil outside, as it would in the ark from the waves.

CHAPTER 17[3]

Why and in what way we ought to flee from the concupiscence of this world, and on the distinction between good thoughts and bad

Let us then understand that there is in us that from which we flee, and that to which we ought to flee—that is, concupiscence and faith, concupiscence which we must flee and faith on which we must lay hold. We must mount up *from* concupiscence, so that as we advance we may leave it behind, and *by* faith, so that by holding fast to it we may be constantly progressing towards better things. Concupiscence has to do with the works of creation, and faith with those of restoration; for by inordinate love for created things we are weakened by concupiscence, and by devout belief in the works of restoration we are made steadfast through faith. And this is why the divine counsels so often cry to us, urging us to flee the world,[4] not indeed in the sense of going away from this visible earth and sky, but in the sense of not continuing in this world's lusts.

And what does it mean to say 'by not continuing'? Who does continue in the desire of the world? He who makes it his soul's delight, he who ever seeks it, continually thinks of it,

[1] Gen. viii, 6 ff.

[2] See Ps. lv, 6–8.

[3] Chapter 17 = MPL, clxxvi, cols. 675–7 (Bk. IV, ch. 8).

[4] See 1 John ii, 15.

sets his heart's intention on it, pursues it by deliberate choice, and in consenting to it finds his pleasure.

Therefore this world is cursed in Holy Scripture and called the enemy of God,[1] not because the world is evil in itself, but because the beauty of the world leads souls astray. For we should not have to flee from the world itself, were not the lust of it evil. So when we flee the lust of the world, we do so because it is evil; but when we flee the substance of the world, we do so not because it is evil of itself, but because it is the occasion of evil. For the lustful mood is born of brooding on the beauty of the world. Hence, if we would turn away from the lust of the world, we must first banish the remembrance of this world from our thoughts. 'In my meditation', says the prophet, 'a fire is kindled.'[2] As logs feed a fire, so do thoughts feed desires. If there have been good thoughts in the meditation, the fire of love is kindled; but if they have been bad, the fire of desire flames up. For as the eye is fed by what it sees, so is the soul fed by what it thinks; and by a shameful sort of traffic the unchaste mind enjoys its desire when it embraces after a fashion the thing that it desires by its thought.

It happens on occasion that what we often think about in an idle sort of way we sometimes come to desire unlawfully; and he who through consenting gets pleasure from the thought is adjudged guilty of the deed. So as the weak in health abstain from certain foods, not because these are bad in themselves, but because they are not suitable for them, so we too ought to keep the sight of earthly things out of our thoughts, not as though those things were evil in themselves, but to prevent our soul, which is weak by its own nature, from being further corrupted by remembering them.

But as far as the things themselves are concerned, everything can be thought about without any sin, for every creature of God is good. Yet again, if we are inclined towards an evil disposition, there is nothing about which we can think, and not sin in so doing. For we can think well about an evil thing, and evilly

[1] See Jas. iv, 4.

[2] Vulg. Ps. xxxviii, 4; cf. A.V. Ps. xxxix, 3.

about a good one, purely of an impure thing, impurely of the pure. For thoughts must be judged, not from the thoughts whence they arise, but from the inclination that gives birth to them. We read of holy men, who not only thought, but also spoke and wrote of impure things; which they most certainly would not have done, if thinking of such unclean things defiled their souls.

What matters is not what you think about, but what sort of inclination issues from the thought. For where evil pleasure does not corrupt the conscience, there thought does not pollute the mind.

But, as we have said, it is expedient for us to forget this world, and to blot out its memory from our hearts; lest maybe if we often think of it, we be inclined towards the lust of it.

We have now, I think, shown sufficiently clearly the origin of the infinite distraction of our thoughts from which we suffer—that is, from the world and from the lust of it, from the works of creation. Again, we have shown by what means our thoughts can be reintegrated—that is, by the works of restoration. And because, as we said above, there can be no order where there is no limit, it remains for us now, having left the works of creation behind us, to seek out the order of our thoughts where they are bounded—that is, in the works of restoration. For this is the matter that we previously proposed for investigation[1]—namely, what the order of our thoughts should be, if they are to enable us to build in ourselves the spiritual house of wisdom. And because thoughts come from things, it is right that the order of the thoughts should be taken from the order of the things.

CHAPTER 18[2]

Of the works of restoration, wherein a threefold order is in divers ways considered, according to the three dimensions of the ark

Turning, then, from the works of creation, as from a flood beneath us from which we have emerged, let us begin to

[1] See Book IV, chapter 1 pp. 122 ff.

[2] Chapter 18 = MPL, clxxvi, cols. 677–8 (Bk. IV, ch. 8–9).

treat of the works of restoration, and with them now go, as it were, into the ark.

The works of restoration, therefore, are all the things that have been done, or that still must be done, for the restoration of man, from the beginning of the world until the end of the age. Among these it behoves us to consider both the things that were done, and the people through and for and among whom they were done, and also the places and the times where and when they were done.

Order in the works of restoration is to be considered in three ways, place, time, and dignity. According to place, as to whether the thing happened near at hand or far away. According to time, as to what was done earlier and what later. According to dignity, as to what is the lowlier and what the loftier. This last is subdivided into many parts, the holy and the holier, the profitable and that which is still more so, the noble and the nobler, the beautiful and the more beautiful, the marvellous and the more marvellous, the rare and the rarer, the difficult and the more difficult, the credible and the more credible, the great and the greater, the dark and the darker, and so forth. And this order which is according to dignity seems to correspond to the height of the ark, as if we were to say that the holy things are reckoned as being in the first storey, the holier in the second, and the very holiest in the third. And similarly with all the other things we have enumerated.

The order of place, however, and the order of time seem to run parallel in almost everything, following the sequence of events. Thus divine providence seems to have arranged that the things which were done in the beginning of time should be done in the east, as in the beginning of the world; and that then, as time moved on towards the end, the climax of events should reach to the west; a fact from which we may conclude that the end of the age is approaching, since the course of events has now reached the end of the world.[1] The first man, consequently, is placed at his creation in the east, in the garden of Eden; so that from that starting-point his posterity may

[1] The Atlantic seaboard was the end of the world for men of Hugh's day.

spread over the whole earth. Again, after the flood the chief of the kingdoms and the head of the world was in the eastern regions, among the Assyrians, the Chaldaeans, and the Medes. Then the supreme power came to the Greeks, and finally, towards the end of the age, it passes to the Romans in the west, as to those who dwell at the world's end.

And just as the sequence of events moved in a straight line from east to west, in the same way the things that happened to right or left—that is, to the north or south—so correspond to what those directions signify that no one giving the matter serious thought could fail to see here the disposition of divine providence.

For instance, to take only a few examples out of many: Egypt is south of Jerusalem and Babylon is north; Egypt means 'darkness'[1] and the south wind is hot. So Egypt signifies this world, that is set in the darkness of ignorance and the heat of carnal concupiscence. And Babylon means 'confusion',[2] and signifies hell, wherein no order dwells, but everlasting dread. And we read that the ancient people of the Hebrews first served in Egypt amid mud and bricks,[3] and then after an interval of many years was led off captive into Babylon.[4] And what else does this fact suggest to us, if not the fall of the whole human race, which, being exiled from its heavenly country through original sin, is first subjected to the vices through its ignorance and lust as long as this life lasts, and then, when that is over, is taken prisoner to the pains of hell—that is, to Babylon, away to the north where the first apostate angel took his seat.[5]

Thus the order of dignity belongs to the height of the ark, the order of time to its length, and the order of place to both its breadth and length. So this passage, 'The kingdom of heaven is like unto a man that is a householder, which went out early

[1] Cf. St. Augustine, *Enarratio in Psalmum lxxvii*, ch. 28 lxxvii, par. 28. (MPL, xxxvi, col. 1001).

[2] Cf. St. Jerome, *Commentarium in Isaiam profetam*, Bk. VI (on Isaiah, ch. 13, verse 1; MPL, xxiv, col. 205D).

[3] See Exod. i, 8–14.

[4] See 2 Kings xxiv, 12–16.

[5] See Isa. xiv, 12 ff.

in the morning to hire labourers into his vineyard, and likewise also at about the third hour, and the sixth, and the ninth, and the eleventh he went out, and seeing others standing sent them into his vineyard',[1] has to do with the length of the ark. This, 'Their sound is gone out through all the earth, and their words to the end of the world',[2] has to do with its breadth. This, 'whither the tribes go up, the tribes of the Lord, unto the testimony of Israel, to give thanks unto the name of the Lord',[3] has to do with its height. And lest I multiply delays by going through each thing individually, I will tell you briefly what still remains to be said.

In these three measurements the whole divine Scripture is contained. For history measures the length of the ark, because the order of time consists in the succession of events. Allegory measures the breadth of the ark, because the fellowship of faithful people consists in their sharing in the mysteries.[4] Tropology measures the height of the ark, because the worth of merits increases with advance in virtue.

CHAPTER 19[5]

A further threefold distinction in the works of restoration, according to the division of the ark into three storeys

There is yet another way in which, if we so wish, we may discern the height of the ark, so that, while the truth remains the same, the expositions of it may be multiplied. For we would have the reader notice this also, that often in this treatise we have presented the same thing in different ways, in order so to enrich our teaching that the wise soul may make trial of every path of knowledge, with this reservation only, that nothing that gainsays the truth be either thought or said. Therefore, as

[1] See Matt. xx, 1–7.

[2] See Ps. xix, 4.

[3] Ps. cxxii, 4.

[4] The most primitive meaning of *sacramentum* is implied here by its connexion with the allegorical sense.

[5] Chapter 19 = MPL, clxxvi, cols. 678–9 (Bk. IV, ch. 9).

the ark is divided into three storeys, so also the works of restoration are divided into three classes. In the first class, as it were in the first storey, is the shadow. In the second class, as in the second storey, is the spirit. Or, if you prefer to use these terms, call the three things figure, actuality, and truth, and understand that the figure and the shadow are the same, the body and the actuality, and the spirit and the truth.

Those things are called shadows, which were done before Christ's coming under the natural and the written law, bodily and visibly, in order to prefigure the things that now, after His coming, are being done bodily and visibly in the time of grace. They are called shadows, because they were both corporal and figures of the corporal. Our sacraments themselves, which are now performed in Holy Church, are called the body. And the spirit is that which the grace of God effects invisibly beneath these visible sacraments. For instance, to take one example, the Red Sea prefigured baptism, which is now sanctified in Holy Church. And the same visible baptism signifies the cleansing from offences, which the Holy Spirit effects invisibly within our souls, beneath the washing of our bodies, in this sacrament.

Thus the Red Sea is the shadow and the figure; the baptism of visible water, which we now have, is the body and the actuality; and the washing away of sins is the spirit and the truth.

CHAPTER 20[1]

A further threefold distinction in respect of the same height

There remains yet another way, of which we spoke just now,[2] by which we can divide the height of the ark. For God performed the works of restoration partly through men, partly through angels, and partly by Himself. So in the first storey we put the works of men, in the second the works of angels, and in the third the works of God.

[1] Chapter 20 = op. cit., col. 679 (Bk. IV, ch. 9).

[2] See Book IV, chapter 10 (p. 136).

Or, if we take it morally, the first storey is faith, the second hope, and the third charity. Or, according to the anagogical sense, the first storey is right thought, the second is wise meditation, and the third pure contemplation. Or, according to active life,[1] the first storey is knowledge, the second discipline, and the third goodness. Or, according to the different states, the first is nature, the second the written law, and the third grace.

If indeed these three are considered from the point of view of time, they measure the length of the ark; if they are assessed according to their dignity, they divide its height. For as they followed each other in time, so did they precede each other in respect of dignity.

CHAPTER 21[2]

A concluding chapter in praise and commendation of the ark

What then is this ark, about which we have said so many things, and in which so many different paths of knowledge are contained? You do not think it is a maze, I hope? For it is not a maze, nor is there toil within, but rest. How do I know this? Because He lives in it who said: 'Come unto Me, all ye that labour and are heavy laden, and I will give you rest . . . and ye shall find rest unto your souls.'[3] For if there is toil where He is, how do those find rest who come to Him? But now 'His place is in peace and His dwelling-place in Sion. There He hath broken the powers of bows, the shield, the sword and the battle.'[4] In the place whence all tumult and disturbance is far off, joy and peace and rest are ever present.

What, then, is the ark like? Do you desire to know? Bear with me, that I may tell you a few things out of many. This ark is like a storehouse filled with all manner of delightful things. You will look for nothing in it that you will not find, and when

[1] I.e. operation as opposed to contemplation.

[2] Chapter 21 = MPL, clxxvi, cols. 679–80 (Bk. IV, ch. 9).

[3] Matt. xi, 28 ff.

[4] Vulg. Ps. lxxv, 3–4; cf. A.V. Ps. lxxvi, 2–3; see Bk. I, ch. 4, n. 3 (p. 50).

you have found one thing, you will see many spread before your eyes. There all the works of restoration are contained in all their fullness, from the world's beginning to its end; and therein is represented the condition of the universal Church. Into it is woven the story of events, in it are found the mysteries of the sacraments, and there are set out the stages of affections, thoughts, meditations, contemplations, good works, virtues, and rewards. There we are shown what we ought to believe, and do, and hope. There the form of man's living and the sum total of perfection are contained. There that which is hidden comes to light, there burdensome tasks seem easy, and matters which might in isolation seem unfortunate, when viewed in their context are seen to be appropriate. There the sum of things is displayed, and the harmony of its elements explained. There another world is found, over against this passing, transitory one; because the things that go through different times in this world exist in that one simultaneously, as in a condition of eternity. There the present does not follow on the past, nor does the future supervene upon the present, but whatsoever is there, is there as in the present.

For this reason also those who dwell there, dwell there always, and always rejoice, grieving for nothing that is past, fearing nothing future, possessing what they love, seeing what they desire; and perhaps that is why the apostle said, 'The fashion of this world passeth',[1] the form of this world, the appearance of this world, the beauty of this world. For there is another world, whose 'fashion' does not pass, nor does its form change, nor its appearance wither, nor its beauty fail. That world is in this world, and this world is less than that world, for that world contains Him whom this world cannot contain. Eyes of flesh see this world, the eyes of the heart behold that world after an inward manner. In this world men have their pleasures, but the delights in that world are ineffable. In this world men run after and applaud vain shows, but in that world they are occupied with inner silence, and the pure in heart rejoice in the sight of the truth.

[1] See 1 Cor. vii, 31.

I meant to speak but briefly, but I confess to you that I am pleased to have much to say; and perhaps there was still more which I might have said, had I not been afraid of wearying you. And now, then, as we promised, we must put before you the pattern of our ark. Thus you may learn from an external form, which we have visibly depicted, what you ought to do interiorly, and when you have impressed the form of this pattern on your heart, you may rejoice that the house of God has been built in you.

NOAH'S ARK: III

(De Vanitate Mundi)

Book I[1]

In which Reason and the Soul converse

I

R. O unclean world, how have we loved you? Is this, then, your fruit? Is this the promise that you make, are these our hopes? Why have we hoped in you? Why have we put our trust in you? Why have we refused to stop and think? Consider how we have been deceived. Nothing is left to us, and we go on our way empty. O unclean world, what is this love that we have given you?

S. What are you seeing, O man?

R. Flight is the best course.

S. I am not clear what you are trying to say. But from your state of stupefaction I perceive that either you are labouring under some severe affliction, or you are seeing something unusual, or else you are turning over some great matter. So do not hide it from me, whatever it may be. For, if it is a danger, you have freed me at the same time. But, if there is no danger and you are disquieting yourself for nothing, I may be able to afford you comfort.

R. Rise up and come and look with me, and I will show you great marvels that are old to the ancients, new to those now living, and subsequent to those as yet unborn.

S. When I really see the thing about which you are speaking, then perhaps I shall understand better what you are trying to say. Now, therefore, show me whither I must come up, in order that I too may see these marvellous things about which you are so perturbed.

R. The loftier the viewpoint of our bodily sight and the higher the place whence it looks out, the wider is its field of vision. Its

[1] *Of This World's Vanity*, Bk. I = MPL, clxxvi, cols. 703–12.

keen perception naturally reaches further when directed from above on things that lie below, when it sees all things so to speak together. But whatsoever it sees in the light by means of its bodily organ, at the same time it darkens in itself in many different ways, even when no outward hindrance intervenes. Sight is restricted in its scope, and it is therefore quite unable to take in very large things; because it is dim, it does not discern those that are very small; and, because it is slow, when it is directed towards distant objects, even though it spans the intervening space, it is impeded by the very distance itself. For it is not sharp-sighted, it does not penetrate inwards, but roves about only over those things that outwardly appear. Moreover it can neither look back to events past, nor forward to those that are yet to come.

I have said this to show you under what limitations this bodily vision labours, since it cannot see a thing that is not planted straight in front of it. And even then, very large objects are beyond it because of their size, the very small elude it by their minuteness, the far-off ones escape it by their distance, and the inward ones are hidden from it by their obscurity. So when you hear yourself invited to 'see', it is not the sight of this eye that I would have you think about. You have another eye within, much clearer than that one, an eye that looks at the past, the present, and the future all at once, which sheds the light and keenness of its vision over all things, which penetrates things hidden and searches into complexities, needing no other light by which to see all this, but seeing by the light that it possesses of itself.

So, because the eye of the flesh is unable to see all at once the things that I am going to show, it is not that eye but the heart's eye that will be needed for this sight. Take your stand in spirit, then, as it were on a watch-tower, and turn your attention on the dwelling-place of the world in all directions, so that everything lies spread before your gaze. And from that vantage-point I will show you everything that you once neither saw nor knew, or that, if you saw it, you had not noticed as you should.

S. I frankly admit that, when the eye of the heart is deliberately opened to see, nothing lies hid from the beholder. On the other hand when I open my bodily eye to see, no matter how plain things are, what I can take in is little enough when compared to the whole. But see, however hard I try to lift my heart, I find that I have so far lived down below in mind as well as in body. For the more I have submitted myself in desire and thought to the contemplation of certain things in this world, the less fitted and the less free have I become for the contemplation of the universe as a whole. Now, therefore, I divest myself of that to which I have previously been clinging, and, as though unburdened of a load laid down, I realize that I have risen above all things. For I cannot tell by what marvellous means it has happened to me that, by being careful to cleave to nothing with particular desire, I am beginning to rise superior to everything by contemplation. Proceed, then, for I now behold the whole world spread before me, and shall see without delay or difficulty whatever you wish to show me.

R. You can see this world, then?

S. Yes, indeed. I have never beheld it so clearly, for never before have I considered it so carefully.

R. How, then, does it appear to you? How does it look?

S. It looks very beautiful. I marvel at such work of God.

R. You find God marvellous in all things; that is already known to everyone. But for the moment, let us say nothing of the works of God. You have not yet begun to marvel at the greatness and quality of these works of men that you behold. For this you should know, that here I am speaking of 'the world' not simply as the manifestation of God's work, but as the mutability of human life in the world. Tell me, therefore, of what nature are the works of men that you behold? How do they strike you?

S. I see great splendour in these too, and when I think what man is, I marvel that he can do such things.

R. If you had properly considered what man is, you would not wonder that he can do such things, but rather that it is in such things that he puts his trust. But the reason why you are filled with such stupid and excessive wonder is because you have not yet begun to consider the dignity of man and the small value of his works.

S. Although what you say is much against my opinion, it could be that I am deceived, and that what you say is true. I want, therefore, rather to listen than dispute. Then if you can prove your point, I shall not have it on my conscience that I withstood you brazenly; and if you cannot do so, no harm will have been done because I wisely held my tongue. Tell me, therefore, what is the dignity of man, and what the trifling value of his work. For in truth, if one looks only at outward appearances, man himself is found to be neither larger than his work, nor fairer in form, nor longer lasting.

R. I want first to discuss with you the works of men. You see them all, their magnitude and quality.

S. They seem great and marvellous enough to me, but you think otherwise, no doubt.

R. I certainly do think otherwise, and I want you to do the same.

S. I am not so obstinate as to be unwilling to be convinced of the truth; so carry on as you please, and I will follow you.

R. Look at all things, and carefully consider them one by one.

S. I am looking and considering, and I am waiting to know what you want to show me out of all these things.

R. What do you see?

S. I see people voyaging at sea. The sea is very calm, the weather very fine, favourable winds are gently blowing too, bearing the ship on its intended course. And all over the ship I see people reclining at feasts and singing to lyre, flute and cithara, soothing the air with every kind of sweet song. The very waters resound with melody, bringing shoals of fish around the ship, which by their frolic make the merrymakers merrier still.

R. What do you make of this?

S. What should I make of it, except that here is great joy, great delight, and—were it only lasting—great felicity.

R. And this is the reason why you like the world?

S. I do not know what reason there is for disliking it.

R. Keep your eye on it a little longer, and do not stop looking until you see the end.

S. I am following them as they go, and waiting to see what happens next.

R. What do you see now?

S. I am afraid to say what yet I cannot hide.

R. What see you, then?

S. I see the sky grow black in all directions, the clouds tossed and driven from their course by the fury of the winds, the sea swelling into billows, and as if hurled aloft from the lowest depths, borne up in one great surge. Alas, what was I praising?

R. What is the matter?

S. Poor wretches, what will become of you in this sea? Why did you put your trust in that deceptive calm? Why, in a precarious situation, were you so carefree? Why were you not suspicious of the smoothness of the sea? Why were you not afraid to trust your lives to the treacherous element? Why did you leave the firmness of the shore? Why did you not travel in safety by land? What profit have you gained from such great danger? See what a trifling benefit you have pursued, and how great a catastrophe you have incurred. And since you would not foresee the true evil that was threatening you, you did not restrain your hearts from the quest of spurious good that was alluring you. O unhappy, wretched men, see how swiftly your joy has been changed, and into what sorry plight your life has fallen. Once, in your foolish rejoicing, you found amusement in the fishes of the sea. Now, when you are shipwrecked and miserably cast away, they receive you as their food.

R. How does it seem to you? Of what quality is this work of man?

S. It is vanity, and vanity of vanities.

2

R. Now turn your attention to something else, and look at that.

S. I have, and I am looking.

R. What do you see?

S. I can see men going on their way, laden with many and great wares. There are countless camels carrying different loads, and many wagons and two-horsed drays in the travellers' train. I can see all kinds of spices and perfumery there, and I discern all sorts of costly clothing, huge heaps of fine metal and every precious stone, horses and mules and slaves, and herds of cattle and sheep without number.

R. Where do you think these people come from, and where are they going?

S. They seem to be coming from some far-off country, and to be conveying all these goods to foreign peoples, to trade for profit. They look like men who are keen and alert, and to judge from their happy appearance, everything is going well with them.

R. What view do you take of this?

S. Well, I can see that their work is arduous enough, but they have the pleasant compensations of variety and the desire for profit for their pains.

R. But just watch, and you will see how much reward they will get for their labours.

S. They have their reward already, if it can but last.

R. Only wait a little. That which is going to happen will come fast enough.

S. They have already gone on further.

R. And what do you see?

S. I see a band of armed men coming out of a pass, and I fear that it may be an ambush.

R. Belated fear will not prevent the suffering.

S. Down they come, as one man, like brigands to seize their prey. And now I see the travellers alarmed and trembling, huddling round their baggage, each snatching up his weapons and awaiting the enemy's attack from a position near his load. They look around in all directions, there is no way of escape open either one way or the other. Every place around is utterly deserted and far from the haunts of men. There is no hope of help. Their foes run up from every side, and make a concerted attack in superior numbers, strong in their greed and bold by reason of the isolation of the place. Why, you poor wretches, do you put up a fight? Why do you offer resistance? Why, in the moment of such desperate danger, are you ready to forfeit your lives and your goods together? Ah, woe is me, I see some are already killed, and others are being robbed, some are falling dead and others are escaping almost naked. But whether those who fall there, or those who flee, are to be counted the more unhappy, I do not know. For some are released from their troubles by death, whereas the rest, in escaping death, are preserved for trouble to come. Whom shall I chiefly mourn, whom shall I more contend with? I will mourn for the dying and I will blame the fugitives. And yet do not the dying justly merit blame for such a death, and for such a flight do not the fugitives deserve that I should mourn them? For avarice has led the former to a miserable death, and a misery greater than death awaits the fugitives from death.

R. How does it strike you? Of what sort is this work of man?

S. It is vanity, and vanity of vanities.

3

R. Turn yet again, and look at something else.

S. I have turned, and I am looking.

R. What do you see?

S. I see a rich man's home.

R. What do you see there?

S. I see an abundance of everything, children growing up, efficient servants, fertile flocks, full barns, storehouses overflowing, health in life, peace in plenty, safety in peace, and happiness in safety.

R. How does it strike you?

S. I see no reason here for grief or fear, yet after the lesson of the previous cases I would not be so rash now as to say that anybody was secure of happiness. I should rather hear from you what I should think.

R. Do you then believe that such a man is happy?

S. I cannot see why not.

R. Which, then, makes a man the happier, to possess much, or to need little?

S. Needing little makes him happier than possessing much.

R. So it is a still happier condition to need little?

S. Clearly.

R. A man is to be reckoned happy, then, not when he possesses much, but when he does not need much.

S. Yet people say a man is happy if he has sufficient means to meet all demands. For they know from experience how depressed a man becomes, if in time of need he is restricted by lack of property.

R. Had you but compared the troubles of the rich with those of the poor, you would realize that the rich man is more unfortunate than the poor. For the more a rich man possesses, the more worry he has. And, above all, because he has to bear the burden of anxiety alone, that which he acquires so eagerly and hoards so carefully is of more benefit to other people than it is to himself. In the fever of his anxiety he tosses unceasingly. He fears the failure of his revenues, for, though his property is great, no less so are the forces at work to dissipate it. He fears the violence of the mighty, doubts the honesty of his own household, lives in perpetual fear of the deceptions of strangers, and, since he knows himself hated by everyone because of his possessions, he tries to avert this by a wretched and unhappy sort of struggle against everyone. And so it comes about that, in cutting himself off from the common fellowship of everyone by this depraved pursuit, he becomes hateful to all men, and a stranger to their love. Moreover, he knows quite well that, if his material prosperity should fail him, he will receive no kindly compassion from anybody else. The worry of his property never leaves him, but the enjoyment of it goes to other people to such an extent that he is often obliged to be generous to those from whom he cannot expect to receive respect, or thanks, or service. As long as he keeps it, they speak ill of him; when he gives it away, they mock him with empty adulation, though he is hurt no less by being laughed at than by being cursed. Always morose, always unhappy, always apprehensive, always weighed down by present cares and troubled by fears for the future, he cannot trust the good fortune that he has, but lives in constant fear of evils that may come. I ask you, then, what real comfort or pleasure can the body have, when the mind is beset with such strains and stresses? What consolation will not be turned into an affliction for the body, when the spirit is wounded by such stings? This is the happiness of the rich man, which you, noticing only its false, superficial advantages, were disposed to extol, because you did not see the real unhappiness within.

S. If this is how things go with a rich man, he who desires great possessions is his own enemy.

R. What, then, is your opinion? How about this as a human activity?

S. This too is vanity, and vanity of vanities.

4

R. Turn now to other things, and look.

S. I have turned, I am looking.

R. What do you see?

S. I see a wedding being celebrated.

R. Well, what about it?

S. There is great rejoicing there, fine apparel, and much splendour. And—not to suppress my opinion—I reckon this more blessed than the other things man does. For this is the thing that, by the bond of love, chiefly makes peace and concord between souls. This displays the advantages of companionship, makes love holy, and protects friendship. Offspring are its fruit, and the increase of our race. It helps us to oppose death's dread necessity, and make good the losses of our fathers in the sons. For what need have I to mention here the fact that in marriage the lust of the flesh, which cannot otherwise be restrained without effort nor yet indulged without shame, is mutually permissible in circumstances so wholesome and modest that chastity itself suffers thereby virtually no loss? For although lust is then permitted its satisfaction, modesty is not put to confusion as a result. Who, then, would think of despising so many and such considerable advantages, unless he were a man who did not see the troubles that ensue from any other course?

R. You would be in a position to assess the benefits of marriage rightly, if you would take into account its disadvantages. For because you are considering only the blessings of marriage, and not its disadvantages, you do not keep a balanced view of them. It cannot be denied that marriage has a number of good points in its favour. But, if we are ready to think the matter out, we shall find the number of trials involved to be even greater. For is there anyone who does not know how rare is that harmony of spirit of which you speak? Nay rather, once the very association that should engender harmony becomes a bore, how quickly does it provide occasions of enmity! And although they disagree with one another, it is not possible for them to part, so that the couple become only the more unhappy in living together. Daily disputes and quarrels consequently become more frequent. Dreadful beatings are the next stage after unkind words. Neither can escape the other; they are obliged to share one home, one table, and one bed, and—what is worse than anything—they have neither a congenial partner nor a separated enemy. For just as to those whose hearts are united in love it does not matter if they be apart in body, so is the physical association a real torment if the couple cannot agree.

With regard, moreover, to the opportunity you took to praise marriage from the fact that it propagates the human race, we grant the truth of what you say, though only in so far as we make it clear that this is not so much the joy of sound health as the salve of debility. For it would have been better for no one alive to die, than for another person to be born to succeed one who dies. But, as it is, some sort of comfort is afforded our misfortune, when the dying, who cannot be detained, are given back to us in the newborn; so that, where we cannot have any who abide for ever, we may at least always have successors.

Let us then support, nay rather, let us preserve this salve for our sorrow, whatever it be, but let us not think of it as a piece of good fortune. Let us praise the draught, though it be not without bitterness that we must drink it, nor without distress that we must rid ourselves of it, since thereby we eject a greater and more dangerous bitterness. If we consider the pleasures of the marriage bed, let us remember also the anguish of child-birth. And, to say nothing for the moment about the other penalties and inconveniences attendant on fleshly pleasure, which weakens the natural forces and diminishes the whole vigour of the body both within and without, who—save one who knows it by experience—can tell what a great labour and trouble it is to have children and, besides other trials better passed over in silence, to suckle them, bring them up, feed them and teach them, forming them in manners and knowledge alike until one brings them through to their majority? Who would not say that they had paid dearly enough for the pleasure even of a single night, when its reward is the trouble and anxiety of so many years? If those who are getting married would only remember this, they would understand that the married state will give them more cause for tears than for laughter. But, for the moment, a little bit of bait for their lust is, as it were, dangled before them, so that they may be caught by the ruthless inevitability of trouble and sorrow. Such is the joy that you are looking at!

S. Not a word of all that you have said can be denied. Your arguments are sound.

R. How then does it strike you? Of what sort is this work of man?

S. This too is vanity, and vanity of vanities.

5

R. Turn yet again, and look at something else.

S. I have turned, I am looking.

R. What do you see?

S. I can see a place of learning, full of pupils. There is a great throng, and I can pick out men of different ages there, boys, lads, young men and old, with differing pursuits as well. Some are learning to school their still unskilled tongues to new elements of speech and the formation of unfamiliar words. Some are trying to learn the inflexions of words by first listening to their regular forms and their cases, and then putting them together and committing them to memory by repeating them over and over again. Some are writing on wax tablets with a style. Others, using their pen with a skilled hand, are drawing designs on parchment in sundry manners and in divers colours. Others again, who with yet keener and more lively zest seem to be exercising themselves in great matters, are testing each other with fallacies and trying to catch each other out in sophistry. Some I see also there who are making arithmetical calculations. Others, plucking stringed instruments, are making music. Yet others are working out various figures and geometrical forms. Some, using special apparatus, are plotting the courses and positions of the stars and the rotation of the heavens. Others are dealing with the nature of plants, the humours of men, and the qualities and properties of everything. And although there is no one method of learning all these things, all are united in their desire to make progress. Nevertheless, call it a busy leisure or an easy busyness as you will, I imagine that, even in your judgement, it is to be preferred to all other human activities, in so far as there is nothing passing here, and nothing base, but the beauty of a wisdom which is eternal is thereby implanted, and its root established, never to be plucked up.

R. An appearance of truth deceives you. It is just the way of this world to wrap up what it designs as a snare for the souls of men in a semblance of truth, lest there should be a chance of their being warned against it. For the easier it is to see when something is wrong, the quicker one is to reject it. But when it puts on the face of truth, it secretly administers a draught of falsehood. Such are these pursuits, pursuits not of wisdom but of human folly, whereby ignorant and foolish men, with a labour as vain as it is obstinate, search out the natures of things while they remain in ignorance of the One who is the Author and Maker of themselves and of all things alike. Yet they do not inquire after Him—as though without God truth might be found or happiness possessed. And, that you may be able to appreciate more clearly still how barren and indeed how pernicious such studies are, you must know that not only do they not enlighten the mind to know the truth, but they actually blind it, so that it cannot recognize the very truth. They capture the heart of a man and as it were draw him out of himself, so that while he is persuaded to take an interest in every other irrelevant matter, he never returns to the consideration of himself. This is the way in which birds are snared when, in the pitch darkness of night, they are shown a light to dazzle them at a place where a net is ready to entrap them.

What, then, does it profit a man to probe carefully into the nature of everything and understand it thoroughly, if he neither remembers nor knows whence he himself comes, nor whither he is going when this life is ended? For what is this mortal life but a journey? For we are passing through, and we see the things that are in this world as it were by the wayside. Does it follow, then, that we should stop and enquire into anything we see as we pass that is unusual or unfamiliar to us, and turn aside from our path for it? This is exactly what the people you are looking at are doing. Like foolish travellers, they have forgotten where they are going and have as it were sat down by the road to investigate the unfamiliar things they see. By habitually giving way to this folly they have already become such strangers to themselves that they do not remember that they are on a journey, nor do they seek their homeland.

S. If this is really as you say, I reckon that the men, whose lives are involved in the sort of deception that deludes not others only but themselves as well, are more wretched than all the rest.

R. That it most certainly is so, is proved by their manner of life and shown by their end. For no life could be more disgraceful and no end more unhappy than to have no hope of salvation when one dies, because one has been unwilling to take the path of virtue while one lived.

S. I frankly admit that it is perfectly absurd to call a person wise when, however much his eyes may be open in regard to other things, he can neither foresee his own ruin, nor take pains to avoid it. But their lewd life and dissolute manners, not to mention their disreputable habits, prove conclusively that such people have neither caution about things present nor foresight in regard to those that are to come.

R. How then does it strike you? Of what sort is this work of man?

S. I see clearly that this too is vanity, and vanity of vanities.

Book II[1]

In which Reason and the Soul continue their conversation

I

R. It is a lengthy business to show the vanity of this world by going through particular cases. You do, however, realize that none of all the things that you are looking at abides. They all pass, and return to the place whence they arose. Just as they all have a beginning, so do they also have an end, though they take different courses and do not all reach their end together in the same way. Some have only lately come to be, others have long since perished, some are only half-way through their course, others at their birth are taking the place of those that existed before; but they are all alike passing away and going towards one place. O mighty flood, whither are you being borne away? Your source is insignificant, you break from a tiny spring, you well up from a trifling conduit. You flow and you grow, you run down and you are engulfed. O stream that fails not, O watercourse never still O whirlpool never sated! Whatever is subject to birth, whatever involves the debt of mortality, that does insatiable death gulp down. It never ceases to consume the one and ensnare the other, or to engulf them both. The present is always passing on, the future always following; and, since the continuity is unbroken, there is a belief that this is the permanent condition of things. For the eyes of mortal men are cast down, and do not look to the course of things in general. Intent upon the small particulars of things, they do not notice what is happening in the world as a whole. Man's life on earth is short, moreover, and his days are spent within a limited environment. His mind, enwrapped in dark-

[1] *Of This World's Vanity*, Bk. II = MPL, clxxvi, cols. 711–20.

ness, is not capable of foreseeing much of the future, or of remembering much of what has gone before; and, when its attention is entirely held by what it sees before it, the continual renewal of the present robs it of the recollection of the past. This is the reason why, when people hear something about the mutability of things, they are forthwith astonished and filled with wonder, as though something novel had occurred; for this topic suggests a new idea to their unheeding minds, though in the world of reality it was long since old enough.

Thus it is that the mutability of the present is a topic that is always old, yet ever new, old to those who through experience or reflection learnt it long ago, new to those who, awakened by experience or admonished by teaching, are just beginning for the first time to know it now. For those yet to come, this knowledge will be reserved for a later period, for they also who come after us will not have this understanding of the world's mutability immediately they begin to have commerce with it, but only after long experience.

Look, then, upon this miserable world, and still more on the wretched folk who love it. This is that which we once believed was friendly to us, the place where we promised ourselves length of days, a quiet life, unruffled peace, and lasting happiness. This is the world whose beauty we loved, whose fairness we praised, whose happiness we longed for, whose glory we desired, and whose joy we embraced. You surely see now how vain it all is, and that it never should be sought for by wise men or lovers of virtue. For where are our fathers? Where are those rich and mighty men, whom once we saw exulting in the glory of this world? Where, when all is said and done, are all those of whose friendship and intimacy we used to feel so sure? See, they have all passed on before us, and we alone are left behind. Let us think now about that world of days gone by, when we were with them and did not yet know what the future held, when we shared with them one purpose and one will, one desire and one habitation, one attachment, one love of life, and one expectation of death. Now they are removed from us and, like forerunners, are sooner departed hence where they were exiles, and sooner come to the place where they are citizens.

If, then, we truly loved them when they were with us, let us prove our love now that they are gone. Let us in desire follow where they are, and long to join them soon and be with them. We show ourselves both faithless and fickle, if for love of things present we forget our former love. O days of old, where are you? Once I loved you and, now that you are gone, I love you yet; nor could your passing ever make me love you less. I loved you, that you might last. Now that you are gone, I love you still, though I do not desire your return. I myself wonder at my desire and consult my feeling, yet I do not understand. For what can I love in you, if I do not wish you to be or choose to have you return? What kind of a feeling is this, so outlandish, so unheard of, that the thing itself should be loved and its presence not? Who shall tell my heart what this love is? I know that I love you, and yet I do not want you to come back to me. So it may be that I do not desire your return because I would rather be with you where you are. Once, then, I loved you falsely, for I loved you where you could not last. Now I love more truly, for now I would be with you where you exist for ever. I am in exile, you are in the homeland. And therefore I never tire of thinking about you, for by remembering and recalling you I myself return somehow in spirit to that home. How sweet it is, when in a foreign land, to remember the days that are gone! The mind is never surfeited with desire, but follows the path of the days that are gone, and sees within itself the way by which it too must pass, the end towards which it is moving, the place to which it must come, the haven where it is to rest.

S. As once, when I thought this world was lasting, its beauty kindled a love of present things in me, so now in a marvellous way its mutability provokes me to desire things to come. By love I am rapt and by desire I am drawn in that direction whither all things go; and I already begin to love the transience of things, for at the sight of the very mutability of everything I burn the more to pass on hence myself. It seems to me that all creation is as it were ready for action, and a clamour, as of the whole of nature, throbs in my ears and exhorts all that has being to hasten to reach their appointed end.

R. So you do realize that everything in this world is frail and passing?

S. Even if I do not, the facts themselves would prove it.

R. What then will happen to those who put their trust in these things?

S. What indeed, except that they will be left idle and empty, when the things they love have passed away?

R. It is good, then, to escape hence and seek a safer dwelling?

S. There is no better course to take. But where, I ask you, shall we go beyond the world, in order to remain unmoved ourselves when all things in the world pass on?

2

R. While this life lasts, you should think of this entire world, because of the mutability of everything, as if it were a flood of down-coursing waters.

S. I see plainly enough that nothing stays still, but that everything goes headlong down.

R. Then think of this world's lovers as shipwrecked people who, being plunged in the depths of this briny ocean, are being dragged under.

S. There could be no better way of putting it. Such are all who love passing things. They go down with the things to which they cling.

R. I take it, however, that you do not doubt that with God nothing passes away, but all things subsist in a changeless eternity.

S. No one doubts that.

R. Behold, then, God as it were in the heights, and this world in the depths. See Him abiding always in the changeless condition of His eternity and, by contrast, this world in the course of its changes as always in a state of flux and instability.

S. That is obvious. Please go on.

R. Now consider the human soul as situated so to speak in between. By a certain native excellence it rises above the mutability below it, but it has not yet attained to that true changelessness that is above it.
S. That is a beautiful and very pleasing way of putting it.
R. If, however, the soul through cupidity immerses itself in all that is borne down in the flood, it is forthwith torn by countless distractions, and, being somehow divided from itself, it is dispersed abroad.
S. How dangerous this inner division is! I should like to know if anyone who is thus distracted can become recollected again.
R. Certainly he can, if he will pick himself up and, shaking off these base attachments, learn to be with himself once more. The more a man gathers himself together in spirit, the more, forsaking lower things, is he raised in thought and desire; until at last, when he comes to that one supreme changelessness, he is altogether unchangeable. . . .[1]

3

S. Just as you made mention of a flood earlier on, it seems to me now that you are going to depict a special sort of ark in the human heart. I confess that this construction seems to me to be very wonderful, the more I think of it; and, although I do not yet know why you embarked on this digression, I imagine that you are trying to clarify something of great importance. It seems that you are presenting me with three ideas that hitherto I had not known or heard of, and which now seem as original as they are wonderful.

The first is the concept of this whole world, with all that is in it, as flood water sweeping past, whose inundations and changing currents—whether we compare them to a flood that covers everything or to a mighty sea—are very like reality.

The second concept is that of the human heart raising itself out of these passing and changeable things, and gradually

[1] Five lines of repetition are omitted.

gathering itself together, so that, when it is nearest to things changeable, it seems like the part of the ark that is borne on the flood below, but, when it draws nearer to things eternal and changeless, then it is integrated and drawn up to a point.

Lastly, in the third and highest place, you represent God as at once the helmsman who steers the ark of man's heart that rides there on the heaving ocean, the anchor that holds it, and the haven that receives it.

So I see these three things, this world like a flood below, the human heart in between like the ark, and, high above, God as the helmsman. This ark excites my wonder, moreover, not only as something quite new, but also by reason of its size. For I see it to be so huge that, while its hull rides on the waters of the flood, its roof reaches up as high as God! Although you did not mention these things without reason, I am longing to know more fully how they are relevant to our discussion. . . .[1]

R. When we want to lift our mind's eye up to things unseen, we ought to have recourse to comparisons with visible things, simply as indications of real knowledge. Thus, when speaking of spiritual and unseen things, something is said to be 'the highest', it is said to be so not as if it were some place above the topmost peak of heaven, but as deepest of all within us. To ascend to God means, therefore, to enter into oneself, and not only to enter into oneself, but in some ineffable manner to penetrate even into one's depths. He, then, who, if I may so say, enters really deeply into himself and, penetrating deep within, transcends himself, he of a truth ascends to God. . . .[2]

S. O saving ark, O happy haven! Blessed is he who can escape this stormy sea unscathed, and come to that tranquillity of rest that knows no equal! I wish I might enter it, I wish I might be saved in it, and be brought through in it! So teach me, I beg of you, how anyone should go into the ark of his own heart, and,

[1] Thirty lines are omitted here, i.e. Müller, p. 40, line 22–p. 41, line 10 = MPL, clxxvi, cols. 714C–715A.

[2] There is an omission here, i.e. Müller, p. 41, line 19–p. 41, line 33 = MPL, clxxvi, cols. 715B–715C.

when he is once in it, what he should do in order to avoid the dangers and attain the haven of the rest that he desires. . . .[1]
R. Very well, I will teach you what you must do. Trample and despise all that is frail and transient, and lo, you have emerged from the flood! Ponder and meditate unceasingly upon the mysteries of your restoration and the blessings of God's loving kindness to you, and you have entered into the ark. And when you let your thought range over the contemplation of the marvellous works of God from the beginning of the world until the end of the age, and weigh what He has done for our salvation, whether under the natural or the written law, or finally under grace, then it is as if you measured in your heart three hundred cubits' length. When also you consider the totality of all believers, it is as if you widened your heart to the width of fifty cubits. When finally by zeal and application you come to understand the knowledge of Holy Scripture, then you lift your heart to thirty cubits' height.

Thus the length of the ark is measured in time, its breadth in numbers, its height in the amount of works. Or again you could think of the length as deeds—that is to say, the historical sense—the breadth as mysteries—that is, the allegorical sense—and the height as virtues—that is, the tropological sense; so that the whole of the Divine Scripture is contained within these limits. But we said many things about these in another book that we wrote about the ark;[2] we must not repeat them all here.

This alone remains, however, that we should enter this saving dwelling, that we may escape the ills that are without, and find therein those delights of God's sweetness that He keeps hid for those who love Him. For this is the house of God and the cellar of wine, into which the King brings His bride, that He may set charity in order in her.[3] Once we have got in there, with the help of God, we shall find it just as easy in that delight

[1] There is an omission here, i.e. Müller, p. 41, line 33–p. 44, line 1 = MPL, clxxvi, cols. 715C–717B.
[2] A reference to *De Arca Noe* or *De Pictura Arcae.*
[3] Song of Sol. ii, 4.

to despise all the pleasures of this world, as to have no fear of adversities in that security.

S. What shall our claim be, to go into God's house?

R. It shall be in the multitude of His mercies.[1]

S. What does it mean, to say 'in the multitude of His mercies'?

R. Because our misery is very great, we need a multitude of mercy. For as often as the mind endeavours to return to itself, and to withdraw both its affections and its thoughts into the secret place of contemplation, it finds the obstacles that bar its entrance to be as many as are the desires of its former life; for the errings and strayings of its old habits will not withdraw and suffer it to be at peace. We must, therefore, beg and implore God's mercy, which moves us forward as often as our misery holds us back from entering on inward peace.

S. Well then, we enter the house of God, but how long do we stay there?

R. We must be in the ark until wickedness be done away, and until the waters of the flood abate. We shall go forth in safety afterwards; for, when this world is ended, there will be nothing more to fear. Then neither will the world without contain anything impermanent, nor will man have anything corruptible within himself.

S. And when we have entered the house of the Lord, what shall we do there?

R. We shall be in perfect peace and gladness. For all who dwell there labour not, nor are they anxious; for there is neither lack of present things nor fear of those to come.

S. If we do not labour, what then shall we do?

R. The one occupation of all who are there is to contemplate God's wonders and to praise Him in His works. And if you will not find it burdensome, I should like to put before you an example, by means of which I could show you clearly how you must conduct yourself in the interior dwelling of the heart.

S. Do so by all means, please. Nothing can possibly be burdensome that brings the longing soul to the achievement of that for which it longs.

[1] See e.g. Pss. v, 7; li, 1; lxix, 13; cvi, 7.

4

R. That inward dwelling which, employing sundry figures, we are wont to call sometimes an ark and sometimes a house, is like the home of a rich householder, and the soul is as the cherished son, who in his father's house is as choicely fed as he is tenderly loved. So we will consider how the child lives in his father's house; for it behoves us to conduct ourselves in the same way in the house of God. For He Himself says: 'Except ye become as little children, ye shall not enter into the kingdom of heaven.'[1]

What, then, does the child do? He is not anxious, neither is he covetous. He busies himself with simple, harmless play. He has such a love of the things at home that, even when he has come into the kingdom, his preference is for the old ways still and he desires his familiar surroundings. He knows his father's property. He runs here and there, now to the field, now to the garden, now to the orchard, the meadows, the fountains, the vines. Every season of the year has its appropriate delights. In spring he follows the ploughmen, in the summer the reapers, and in autumn he goes out with those who harvest the grapes. Everywhere he finds sustenance, everywhere mirth, everywhere refection, everywhere delight; and besides the daily family meals with which he is fed at home, he is even sometimes brought back to his former pleasures by sharing the servants' fare out of doors. He delights to pluck the newly ripened fruits, to rub out the ears of corn, roasted while the grains are still unripe, and to select the ripening clusters of grapes. He looks for the little birds' nests, and takes home with great delight and joy the eggs or the young ones that he finds. Though it be little enough, he seeks his food from his own hunting, rather than from other men's abundance.

If he happens to know that his father is off to some village or castle, whether to market or to a feast, and coming back next day, he desires to go with him, and see new and unusual sights, so that, on his return, he can tell his friends what he has

[1] Matt. xviii, 3.

seen, what fashions men are wearing, how the country lies, how big the towns are, how high the houses are, what quantity of goods there is for sale, what he found, what he bought, and what he has brought back. He is glad, therefore, to go out sometimes, since he will be coming back. But should someone compel him to go into an exile from which he could never hope to return, he would not leave his father's house without great grief and sorrow for his homeland. He goes out gladly, then, so that he may come back. He sometimes wants to see what is going on abroad, that he may come home the richer, and refreshed. But he does not want to make any permanent home except in his father's house and household, among whom he was born and reared. He wants to live with them and to grow old among them. He does not want to be separated from them even in death, so that, even when he is dying, he may not forsake those living beings whom he has known and loved. This company, this dwelling-place, these pleasures and this joy, all these he would have always. He seeks for nothing more, he covets nothing further.

Let us then study to behave in the Lord's house in the same way, and we shall find peace equally with rest and joy. Let us be simple, not covetous of other people's things, but loving those delights which God has prepared for us, and which are found in His House, more than the pleasures of the world. Let us engage our heart and gladden our soul and kindle our affections ceaselessly with these. There we have limpid springs, there we have flowery meadows, level spacious plains, fruitful vineyards, fertile flocks, abundant harvests, fruitful orchards, watered gardens, and all manner of delights that the mind can rightly seek or happily possess.

S.[1] Please tell me more expressly what these particular pleasures are that you enumerate.

R. Fruitful trees are righteous men, who afford a pattern of good works for us to feed upon. Springs are wise men, plains humble ones, vineyards those who cultivate themselves with

[1] Müller omits this question.

discipline, and meadows verdant with sundry virtues are those who refresh others with the harvest of their toil and, by drawing others to the faith by word and example, increase the number of the flock as if they gave it birth.

5

R. These are the delights that we have in the house of God from without, leaving aside those incomparable banquets with which mothering grace daily feeds and refreshes us within doors. Let us therefore go in, and the Lord will be our leader, to guide our steps in the paths of His commandments; so that, remembering His mercies which are from everlasting, we may stir up our hearts to His love and kindle our desires. But, when we have entered, I will go first and lead you from the front of the house into the inner rooms. We will wander round through all the rooms and throughout its length and breadth and height, and we will climb from floor to floor, and will not cease until we come to the King's throne. We will take a walk through all the works of our restoration from the beginning of the world, taking the things that happened and the deeds of men according to the successive periods of time.

And when we have beheld the things that are inside, from time to time I shall open the window of the ark and, as an alternative, we shall refresh our mind's eye by looking out on what is going on in the waters of the flood. For it will be pleasanter first to look from our vantage point at the evils which we have escaped, and then, turning our eyes to the good things within, to remember what we have found, and what we possess.

S. We shall love those good things better, if by this alternation we are careful always to remember our misery and danger too, and to take warning therefrom.

R. Very well, then. Your part shall be to ask as many questions as you like and deem worth the asking about the wonderful things that you have seen, whether inside or out. And mine shall be to answer your questions as far as I am able. But first let me bring you into the front of the house, that is, the prow, which reaches to the east; so that our entrance may be at the same time from the beginning of the world and from the beginning of the age. For because the length of the house is three hundred cubits, the fore end reaches to the east, and the after end to the west. The left side, however, looks to the south and the right side to the north, because the providence of God has so ordered the course of events that the things which were done in the beginning of the age should be in the east, as at the beginning of the world, and that at length, when the times had rolled on towards the end of the age, the completion of all things should come down in the west—that is, at the world's end. Therefore the first man, after he was created, was placed in paradise, in the eastern quarter; so that thence, as from the world's beginning, the entire stock of mankind might flow forth over all the lands.

Thereafter, the chief among the kingdoms was Assyria, in the east, but in the later periods of the age the supreme power passed to the Romans, who dwelt in the west.

As we begin from the origin of all things and go along the length of the ark through the works of restoration to the end and consummation of all things, we shall find a path that takes us through the midst of the years; so that, as we pass along, everything to north or south—that is to say, to left or to right—will be visible on either hand, as if it were outside the ark in the flood.

This will be a long walk, but not a tedious one, for manifold delight in such great things will meet us on our way. Again, those who peer out from the window, their eyes searching far and wide from the safe stance in the high look-out, see spread out before them such an amazing confusion and state of flux in the world.

S. Now we are entering at the beginning of the world. But as far as I am concerned, when I set out to turn my gaze backwards as it were beyond the world, desiring to know what was before the ages, I see nothing at all.

R. Your questions start from a remote beginning.

The Soul's Three Ways of Seeing[1]

' "Vanity of vanities," said the Preacher, "all is vanity" '

Now where do you suppose that this man's mind was, when he said all this? He was certainly a man, yet he was above men. For, had he not been above men, he would not have seen that all men are liars. This is why we, when we come to these reflections, must ourselves first reflect, and differentiate between the kinds of spiritual sight. Thinking, meditating, and contemplating are the rational soul's three ways of seeing.

Thinking occurs when the mind becomes aware of things passing through it, when the image of some real thing, entering through the senses or rising up out of the memory, is suddenly presented to it.

Meditation is the concentrated and judicious reconsideration of thought, that tries to unravel something complicated or scrutinizes something obscure to get at the truth of it.

Contemplation is the piercing and spontaneous intuition of the soul, which embraces every aspect of the objects of understanding.

Between meditation and contemplation there appears to be this difference: meditation always has to do with things that are obscure to our intelligence, whereas contemplation is concerned with things that are clear, either of their nature or in relation to our intellectual capacity. Again, while meditation is always exercised in the investigation of one matter, contemplation embraces the complete understanding of many, or even of everything. Meditation is, then, a certain inquisitive power of the soul, that shrewdly tries to find out things that are obscure and to disentangle those that are involved. Contemplation is the alertness of the understanding which, finding everything plain,

[1] This passage from Hugh's unfinished commentary on *Ecclesiastes* = MPL, clxxv, cols. 116–18.

grasps it clearly with entire comprehension. Thus in some ways contemplation possesses that for which meditation seeks.

There are, however, two kinds of contemplation. That which comes first and is proper to beginners, consists in the consideration of created things; the other, which comes later and is proper to the mature, consists in the contemplation of the Creator. In the Book of Proverbs, Solomon begins as it were at the stage of meditation. In Ecclesiastes, he rises to the first degree of contemplation. In the Song of Songs, he betakes himself to the highest.

In meditation, a sort of wrestling-match goes on between ignorance and knowledge, and the light of truth somehow flickers in the midst of the darkness of error. It is then rather like fire in green wood, which gets a hold at first only with difficulty; but, when it is fanned by a stronger draught and begins to catch on more fiercely, then we see great billows of black smoke arise, and smother the flame, which so far is still only fairly bright and leaping out here and there, until at last, as the fire gradually grows, all the smoke clears, the darkness is dispelled, and a bright blaze appears. Then the conquering flame, spreading throughout the crackling pyre, gains ready mastery and, leaping round the fuel, with lightest touches of its glancing tongues consumes and penetrates it. Nor does it rest until, reaching the very centre, it has so to speak absorbed into itself everything that it had found outside itself.

But once that which was to be burnt up has been devoured by the fire, and so has been entirely transmuted from its own nature into the nature and the likeness of the fire, then all the noise dies down, the roar is hushed, the darting flames are withdrawn, and that fierce, greedy fire, having brought everything beneath its own control and bound it up together in a sort of friendly likeness to itself, sinks down in deep peace and silence. For it no longer finds anything other than itself, nor anything in opposition to itself.

The fire, then, appeared at first in flame and smoke, then in flame without smoke, and lastly as pure fire, without flame or smoke. Even so the carnal heart is like green wood which has not yet had the sap of fleshly concupiscence dried out of it. If it should conceive a spark of the divine love or fear, at first the smoke of its passions and fears arises, because of the resistance of its wrong desires. Then, when the mind is strengthened with the flame of love and this begins to burn more steadily and shine more brightly, all the darkness of its upheavals quickly disappears, and then the soul, with a pure heart, gives itself over to the contemplation of the truth. And finally, when diligent beholding of the truth has pierced the heart, and it has entered with its whole desire totally into the very fount of truth supreme, then, being as it were completely set on fire with the sweetness of the same, and itself transmuted into the fire of love, it sinks down to rest in utter peace from every conflict and disturbance.

In the first stage, then, since right counsel must be sought amid the perils of temptations, there is in meditation as it were smoke and flame together. In the second, since the heart's attention is given purely to the contemplation of the truth, there is at the beginning of contemplation so to speak flame without smoke. At the third stage, since the truth has now been found and charity made perfect, nothing but the one thing is sought; in the pure fire of love, with the utmost peace and joy, the soul is gently beaten back. Then, the whole heart being turned into the fire of love, God is known truly to be all in all. For He is received with a love so deep that apart from Him nothing is left to the heart, even of itself.

In order, therefore, to distinguish these three things by proper names, the first is meditation, the second admiration, and the third contemplation. In meditation, the inopportune disturbance that arises from the fleshly passions clouds the mind that a loving devotion has enkindled. In admiration, the novelty of the unwonted vision lifts up the soul in wonder. In contemplation, the taste of a wondrous sweetness changes everything to joy and gladness.

In meditation, therefore, there is care, in admiration wonder, in contemplation sweetness. Yet even a true spiritual admiration can refresh the heart with a great gladness when, after the struggle with temptations and the darkness of error, it suddenly composes the soul in an unlooked-for state of peace, and floods it with an unaccustomed light. In this light, therefore, being rapt in spirit above all transient and perishable things, this man perceived that, among all that is, there is nothing that lasts, and, as if stricken with fear at this new and unfamiliar sight exclaimed, 'Vanity of vanities, all is vanity'.

Of the Nature of Love[1]

We daily drop some word respecting love lest, if we do not heed it, its fire perhaps should kindle in our hearts and burst into a flame, whose property is either to consume or purify a thing entire. For all that is good derives from it, and from it every evil comes. A single spring of love, welling up within us, pours itself out in two streams. The one is the love of the world, cupidity; the other the love of God, charity. The heart of man is in fact the ground from which, when inclination guides it towards outward things, there breaks that which we call cupidity; although, when its desire moves it towards that which is within, its name is charity.

There are, then, two streams that issue from the fount of love, cupidity and charity. And cupidity is the root of every evil, and charity the root of every good. So all that is good derives from it, and from it every evil comes. Whatever it may be, then, it is a great force in us, and everything in us derives from it, for this is why it is love.

But what is love, and how great? What is love, and whence? The Word of God also discusses this. Is not this a subject rather for those who commonly debase love and decency? See how many there are who gladly take up the question of its mysteries, and how few who are not ashamed to discuss it in public! What, then, are we thinking of? Perhaps in an excess of wantonness we wear a harlot's face, since we are not ashamed to compose something in writing about love, though these are matters that even the shameless are sometimes unable to express in words without a blush. Yet it is one thing to delve into vice in order to root it out, and another to incite to what is vicious, that truth and virtue be not loved. Our purpose is to probe and

[1] *De Substantia Dilectionis* = MPL, cxlvi, cols. 15–18 (*Institutiones in Decalogum*, ch. IV).

seek that we may know and—when we know—avoid that into which some others go that they may know and, knowing, may indulge therein—namely, what it is in us that divides our desires in so many ways and leads our hearts in different directions.

Now we find that this thing is nothing else but love which, as a single movement of the heart, is of its nature one and single, yet is divided in its act. When it moves inordinately—that is, whither it should not—it is called cupidity; but, when it is rightly ordered, it is termed charity. How, then, can we define this movement of the heart that we call love? It will be worth our while to look more closely at this movement from which, when it is evil, so many ills proceed and, when it is good, so many blessings come, lest to some extent it should elude us and remain unknown and consequently unavoided when it is evil and, when it is good, unsought and undiscovered. Let us, therefore, go into this matter of its definition and think about it; for the object of our inquiry is a hidden matter, and the deeper it lies, the more it controls the heart in either direction.

Love, then, appears to be, and is, the attachment of any heart to anything, for any reason, whether it be desire or joy in its fruition, hastening towards it by desire, tranquil in its enjoyment. Here lies your good, O heart of man, here also is your evil; for, if good you be, your good can have no other source; nor can your evil, if it is evil that you are, except in that you love that which is good rightly or wrongly, as the case may be. For everything that exists is good; but, when that which is good is wrongly loved, the thing in itself is good, but the love of it is bad. So it is not the lover, nor what he loves, nor the love wherewith he loves it that is evil; but it is the fact that he loves it wrongly that is altogether evil. Only set charity in order, then, and there is no evil left.

It is our desire, if only we be equal to the task, to persuade you of an important fact. Almighty God, who lacks for nothing because He is Himself the supreme and true Good, He who can neither receive increase from another, since all things come from Him, nor suffer a personal loss that could cause Him to fail, since in Him all things live unchangeably, this God created the rational spirit by no necessity but out of love alone, in order to bestow on it a share in His own blessedness. That it might, moreover, be fitted to enjoy such bliss, He put love in it, a certain spiritual sense of taste, as it were, to relish inward sweetness, so that through that very love it might savour the happiness of its true joy and cleave to it with unwearying desire.

By love, then, God has joined the rational creature to Himself, so that by ever holding fast to Him it might as it were by its affection suck, by its desire drink, and by its joy possess in Him the good that would make it happy. Suck, little bee, suck and drink the sweetness of thy Sweet that passes telling! Plunge in and take thy fill, for He can never fail unless you first grow weary. So cleave to Him, abide in Him, receive Him and have joy of Him. If appetite be everlasting, everlasting too shall be the blessedness. Let us no longer be ashamed or regretful for having spoken about love. Let us not be regretful where there is such profit; where there is such loveliness, let us not be ashamed.

By love, therefore, the rational creature is brought into fellowship with his Maker; the bond of love is the one link that binds the two in one, and the stronger the bond the greater the blessedness. This is also the reason why, in order to extend that undivided union and perfect concord in both directions, the link is doubled in the love of God and of one's neighbour; to the intent that by the love of God all might come together into one, while by the love of their neighbour all might be joined to each other. In this way, each might through love of his neighbour possess more fully and completely in another that which he could not lay hold of in himself of the One to whom all adhere, the good of all becoming in this way the sum of individual possession.

Set charity in order, then. What does this mean, 'set charity in order'? If love be desire, let it make real haste; if it be joy, then let it rest indeed. Love is, as we have said, the attachment of any heart to any thing for any reason, desire in the longing for it and joy in its fruition, hastening towards its object in desire, at rest in its enjoyment, running to it and resting in it. Towards what, and in what? Only listen, and perhaps we can explain whither our love should run and wherein it should rest.

There are three things that can be loved either rightly or wrongly, namely, God, one's neighbour, and the world. God is above us, our neighbour is our equal, the world is below us. So set charity in order. When it runs, let it run rightly; when it rests, let it rest aright. It is desire that runs and joy that rests. Hence joy is always one and the same, for it is always about one thing and cannot alter with any change. But desire is subject to change, and therefore it does not confine itself to one matter, but assumes various forms. For whenever we are running, we are running either *from* some desire, or *with* some desire, or else *in* some desire for some object.

How, then, should our desire run? God, our neighbour, the world, those are the three possibilities. When our desire sets out, only let God be in it in three ways, our neighbour in two, and the world in one, and then in our desire, charity is set in order. For love, as desire, can run aright both from God, and with God, and unto God. It runs from God when it receives from Him the power that enables it to love Him. It runs with God, when it in no respect gainsays His will. It runs to God, when it seeks to rest in Him. As far as God is concerned, these are the three ways of desiring.

Those that concern our neighbour are two. For desire can run from one's neighbour (and with him), but it cannot run unto him. Desire can run from our neighbour, as rejoicing in his salvation, and with him as wishing to have him as a fellow-traveller on the road to God and a companion when the goal is reached. But to run unto him, as placing its hope and trust in man, that it cannot do. As far as our neighbour is concerned, these are the two ways of desiring—that is to say, as running from him or with him, but not unto him.

Only one thing pertains to the world, namely to run from it, but not either with it or towards it. Desire runs from the world when, seeing the outward works of God, it turns itself more ardently to Him within, in wonder and in praise. It would run with the world, if it conformed itself to this present world with the changes of the times, being cast down when things go ill, or elated when they go well. It would run to the world, if it wanted always to rest in its delights.

Set charity in order, then, that desire may run from God, and with God, and unto God, from our neighbour and with him, but not to him, from the world, but neither with nor unto it. And let it find its rest in the joy of God alone; for, if it is true joy, then love is resting rightly; if it is true desire, then love is running rightly. For love, as we have said, is the attachment of any heart to any thing for any reason, desire in its longing for the thing and joy in its fruition, running to it and resting in it. This is charity set in order, and all that we do apart from this is not ordered charity, but inordinate cupidity.

Select Bibliography

(Full references for the period down to 1957 will be found in the Index bibliographique of R. Baron, *Science et Sagesse chez Hugues de St. Victor* (Paris, 1957), pp. 231–63. Here only a selection relevant to the subject-matter of the volume is given.)

I. SOURCES

Hugonis de S. Victore Opera Omnia, ed. J. P. Migne, *Patrologia Latina*, vols. clxxv, clxxvi, clxxvii. (This edition, which is a reprint of the Rouen edition of 1648, must be used with the aid of the modern criteria of authenticity cited below under Secondary Authorities*. It should also be noted that in several matters the printing of 1879 is inferior to that of 1854.)

De Arrha Animae and *De Vanitate Mundi*, ed. K. Müller, in *Kleine Texte für Vorlesungen und Übungen*, 123 (Bonn, 1913).

Didascalicon de Studio Legendi, ed. C. H. Buttimer (Washington, 1939).

The Soul's Betrothal-Gift (*De Arrha Animae*), trans. F. S. Taylor (London, 1945).

The Divine Love (*De Laude Caritatis* and *De Amore Sponsi ad Sponsam*), trans. a Religious of C.S.M.V. (London, 1956).

On the Sacraments of the Christian Faith (*De Sacramentis Christianae Fidei*), trans. R. J. Deferrari (Cambridge, Mass., 1951).

II. SECONDARY AUTHORITIES

BARON, R.

*'Etude sur l'authenticité de l'oeuvre de Hugues de St. Victor', *Scriptorium*, 10 (1956), pp. 182–220.

Notes biographiques sur Hugues de St. Victor, *Rev. Hist. Ecclés.* 51 (1956), pp. 920–34.

Science et Sagesse chez Hugues de S. Victor (Paris, 1957).

BONNARD, F.

Histoire de l'abbaye de S. Victor (Paris, 1904), vol. 1.

CHATILLON, J.

'De Guillaume de Champeaux à Thomas Gallus', *Revue du Moyen Age Latin* (1952), pp. 139–272.

'Une ecclésiologie médiévale: L'idée de l'église dans la théologie de l'école de S. Victor au XIIe siècle', *Irénikon*, XXII (1949), pp. 115–38; 394–411.

CHENU, M. D.

La théologie au douzième siècle (Paris, 1957).

CONGAR, Y.

'Ecclesia ab Abel', *Abhandlungen über Theologie und Kirche: Festschrift für Karl Adam* (Dusseldorf, 1952), pp. 79–108.

CROYDEN, F. E.

Notes on the life of Hugh of St. Victor, *Journal of Theological Studies*, 40 (1939), pp. 232–53.

DICKINSON, J. C.

The Origins of the Austin Canons and their introduction into England (London, 1950).

*EYNDE, D. van den

Essai sur la succession et la date des écrits de Hugues de S. Victor, *Spicilegium Pont. Athen. Anton.* (Rome, 1960).

GHELLINCK, J. de

Le mouvement théologique du XIIe siècle, (2nd ed., Bruges, 1948).

LASIC, D.

Hugonis de S. Victore, Theologia Perfectiva (Rome, 1956).

*LOTTIN, O.

Quelques recueils d'écrits attribués à Hugues de St. Victor, *Recherches de Théologie ancienne et médiévale*, 25 (1958), pp. 248–84.

LUBAC, H. de

Exégèse Médiévale (Paris, 1961), 2ème partie.

MARTÈNE, E.

De antiquis ecclesiae ritibus (Antwerp, 1737), vol. 3, cols. 701–840 (an edition of the *Antiquae consuetudines S. Victoris*).

SMALLEY, B.

The Study of the Bible in the Middle Ages (2nd ed., Oxford, 1952).

TAYLOR, J.

The origin and early life of Hugh of St. Victor: an evaluation of the tradition, *Texts and Studies in the History of Medieval Education*, no. 5 (University of Notre Dame, 1957).

VERNET, F.
Hugues de S. Victor, *Dictionnaire de théologie catholique*, vii (1922), cols. 240–308.

WILMART, A.
Opuscules choisis de Hugues de St.-Victor, *Revue Bénédictine*, 45 (1933), pp. 242–8.

Index

Works other than those of Hugh of St. Victor will be found under authors' names.

Modern writers are indexed under surnames; other authors under the Christian name.

Only a selection of the more important doctrinal themes and technical terms appears in the index.

INDEX